HOW TO DEVELOP YOUR PSYCHIC POWERS

The ultimate goal for each of us is to be more informed, more positive, more successful in our relationships and our financial circumstances. Through the power of our psychic abilities, we can strive to make choices which are important for our happiness and success in all areas and for increased benefit and productivity to others and our selves.

HOW TO DEVELOP YOUR PSYCHIC POWERS

Art and Science of Psychic Healing

LARRY M. MCDANIEL
PHYLLIS G. MCDANIEL

New Age Books

ISBN: 978-81-7822-326-1

Revised Edition: Delhi, 2008
First Edition Delhi: 2001

Published by
NEW AGE BOOKS
A-44 Naraina Phase-I
New Delhi-110 028 (INDIA)
Email: nab@vsnl.in
Website: www.newagebooksindia.com

Printed in India
at Shri Jainendra Press
A-45 Naraina Phase-I, New Delhi-110 028

Preface

As a therapist of more than twenty years experience, I have encountered problems within people that others have only heard about or read about in psychology texts. I have dealt with reincarnation, possession, the law of Karma and many other areas of concern. I have witnessed tremendous trauma inflicted by well-meaning organizations as well as personal traumas and personal relationship problems. People are searching for meaning and purpose in their lives and have resorted to many avenues in this search.

Our society is peppered with groups and individuals promoting destructive chemicals and illegal drugs that are available to those in search of values in life but who mistakenly go down the wrong road and wind up in a regressive rather than progressive situation. The deep inner search is what this book is dedicated to and what inner revelations are all about. The student will experience a new awareness and renewed purpose that was only dreamed of previously.

What the student will learn in this book is based upon sound principles that I have discovered over a twenty-year period and condensed into precise techniques that work and work well. These techniques will enhance the student's understanding of the truth concerning extra-sensory perception and a new level of internal awareness will be revealed that absolutely astounds most neophytes on the path of enlightenment. The student will become aware of just how valuable he or she is in this universe as a human being with the potential to ascend into the greatest degree of inner awareness he or she has ever known.

Much of the Western world's problem is that we tend to give credence only to that which we can touch, see, feel or observe in a material sense, and we tend to ignore that which is within us. People can't envision that they have the same abilities that seers of old had, and they only need to develop them to realize it.

Open your mind to new methods, open your sensitivities to new experiences and be prepared to see an entirely new world and undergo magnificent revelations of the world we live in.

Contents

PART I

TECHNIQUES FOR PSYCHIC READING

CHAPTER 1

What is a "Psychic Reading"?

The term "Psychic" is defined by Webster as a person apparently sensitive to non-physical forces. Within the context of this definition we can deduce that someone who is "Psychic" can perceive impressions without the normal physical channels that we are accustomed to. Someone who is "Psychic" may claim to receive ideas, thoughts or impressions from some distance in proximity, past or future time or to be aware of things through or around other people without any known method of physical perception.

This book will deal with techniques that are designed to be utilized by the student in order to obtain psychic perceptions. It is also designed to enable the student to organize them into a sensible arrangement whereby he or she can interpret what is seen and relate it to others in a sensible and understandable manner. The student will be enabled to separate his or her own thoughts, images, perceptions or preferences from those that are external to himself or herself.

Utilizing the techniques found in this book, the student will be able to give another person a well-rounded reading with an accuracy of better than 80-90%. The subject who is being given the reading can determine the accuracy. Accuracy is dependent upon the reader's ability to properly interpret the images and impressions that are received.

The more time the student puts into practice of the principles taught herein, the greater will be the student's ability to achieve success in image interpretation and, subsequently, his client's satisfaction. It is the goal of the student to be 100% accurate in all of his or her readings.

Mind Framing

The term "Mind Framing" will sometimes be utilized to describe the process of using a certain technique. The mind frame is the process of picturing a certain setting, much as a movie setting, in order to allow selected things to be seen, placed or manipulated in order to obtain additional information which otherwise would not be available.

One such mind frame will be for the student to picture lovely red velvet flocked wallpaper with an oval in the center. This mind frame will be utilized for the perception of loved ones, personal fulfillment, close friends, etc. This will be fully explained further on in the course.

The main function of the mind frame is to allow the reader to get into a mental attitude of being in close association with his subject's ideas of things and to be able to structure a mental picture wherein impressions will be discernible which are not of the reader's own making.

Mind frames are much like painting a background scene and allowing the players to enter the scene. The players will enter a scene of tranquility when peaceful background pictures and images are already put into place and the overall mood is receptive. This will be taught in the course. Mind frames can be considered as "props".

Mental Posturing

The term "Mental Posturing" will be used from time to time

to describe the particular state of mind that is helpful to obtain certain types of information. When giving a reading, the reader must adapt to certain "attitudes" wherein he is receptive to the images or ideas which may be apparent. The reader must adopt a mental posture of openness and expectation when seeking information concerning another person.

When reading about another person's past experiences, the reader should adopt a mental posture of being "matter of fact" and describe what he sees just as he sees it. In discussing the subject's personal fulfillment, the reader should adopt a posture of concern, sensitivity and caring. The appropriate postures, or attitudes, will enhance the reading process and produce maximum accuracy. Proper posturing will relax the subject and instill confidence in his mind concerning his reader. The more relaxed and cooperative the subject, the better will be the quality of your reading.

Additionally, it is far better to begin a reading with no previous information or discussion with your subject. The more discussion with the subject prior to the reading, the greater the chance of getting personal impressions mixed up with the ones received while performing the actual reading. I personally prefer that the subject does not say anything until I am well into the reading and then only for guidance from him or her concerning the reasons why he or she wanted the reading. Proper mental posturing will come with experience.

I much prefer to read people whom I have never met. Friends, relatives and acquaintances generally make for less than accurate results because of prior information and personal preferences and feelings. You can be objective only when you don't know the person you are reading.

Overall Summation

To give psychic readings is to give an honest, open and unbiased picture of your impressions to your subject. You have to be honest and tell just what you see. To interject personal beliefs, prejudices or other emotions into your reading is to erode the credibility of your readings, and you do an injustice to your subject. I always reveal what I see even if it isn't good. The only thing I will not reveal is death.

If I am giving a reading and I see an end to my subject's lifeline, I absolutely will not tell him. To tell someone that he is going to die can bring about a self-fulfilling prophecy. You must always remember that your subject can change anything you predict for the future. We all have free will and can consciously change our future by our present actions. It, therefore, behooves you to be honest in your reading and inform the people of what you see and anticipate based upon their present situation and circumstances. I always impress upon the subjects that they have the ability to change any prediction I may make. I can give them what is indicated in the images I see. I can also tell them how to change some of the things for their future if they so desire.

If my subject requests the health condition of a close friend or relative, depending upon the circumstances, I may tell him of an impending death but not a personal death revelation. This is something I just don't do. There was a lady who asked me about her father who was old and had cancer. She wanted to know how long her father was going to live. I gave her my interpretation of her father's lifeline. I saw the line declining and estimated that he wouldn't last beyond three months. It depends upon the circumstances as to whether I will even reveal the death of a close friend or relative.

I also wish to emphasize that once you have made a statement, stick with it. Don't go back and change your reading or change your interpretation in any way. I have known of readers who have made predictions and then backtracked on them and made excuses. If you perform a reading on someone, tell him what you see. Even if your subject objects, cannot associate or relate to what you are describing in some manner, don't change your reading. I have had many occasions in the past when I have described someone to a subject, and the subject denied knowing anyone who fit the description only to have him call me later and relate that he had remembered the person whom I had described. Many people have told me that what I predicted for them would be impossible and that there would be no possible way for it to come to pass. They, too, have called and related that the events happened exactly the way I had revealed it to them and were quite amazed that this had occurred.

One young lady was given a reading wherein I told her that she would meet a gentleman of a certain description in about three months. She was involved in a relationship at that time and could see no reason why she would meet anyone else. She called back a few months later and revealed that she and her former fiance had broken up and she had met a new person recently who matched the description of the man I had foreseen, and she had met him three months after the reading.

Don't be afraid of your predictions of the future and don't back off from your visions of the past or present regarding your subject. The techniques you will soon be taught are valid and strong tools. They will absolutely work for you and can be validated by your subjects as to their accuracy. You will not have to make any excuses for your revelations or predictions.

CHAPTER 2

Reading Techniques

Hand Temperature Measurements

The first technique that I use to get into harmony with my subject is known as the "Hand Temperature Measurement". This particular technique isn't a true psychic perception but prepares you for establishing rapport with your subject and getting into the proper mental posture for the true psychic reading that will soon follow.

Refer to diagram "A", and please note the position of the hands. Your fingertips are to rest directly in the palm of your subject's hand, and the subject's fingertips are to rest directly in your palm. The fingers of your hand and your palm are the only areas of physical contact that you will have with your subject. It doesn't matter which hand you hold or if you hold both hands in this manner. The most important thing is that your subject's hands be free of the effects of hot or cold drink cups, winter chill or anything artificial in regard to their temperature.

DIAGRAM "A"

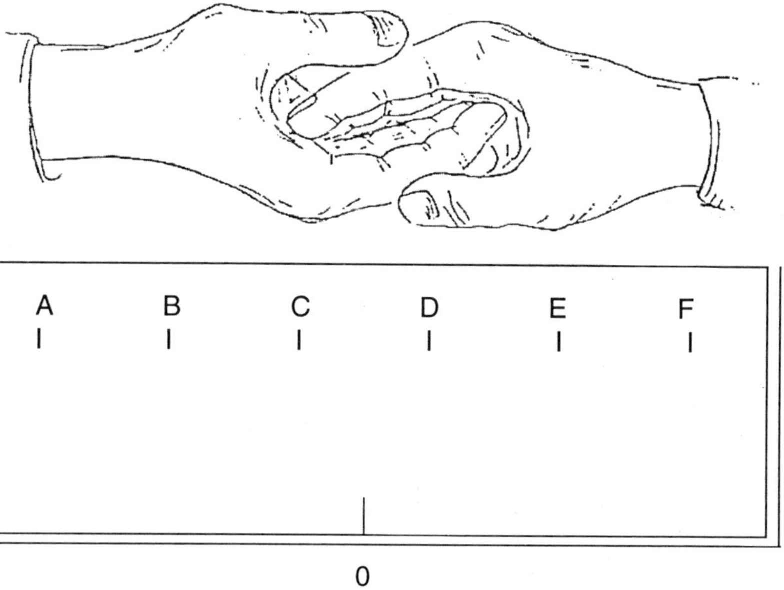

(a) Total Emotionality

This person's heart rules his head. He is totally emotionally oriented. Whatever he/she feels right is what he or she will do. Such a person thinks after and not before and is very warm-hearted.

(b) Emotional control but some Reserve

This person is still ruled by the heart but with some caution. The degree of caution is not enough but can be enhanced for greater intellectual control of emotional involvement.

(c-d) Balance between Emotional and Intellectual Rule

This person tends to be able to intellectually reason things out before leaping into situations. when something feels right to him (C) and thinks out OK, he will move. For this person, the head and heart must agree before he will take action.

(e) Intellectual Control

This individual will reason things out before making a plunge. It has to be the proper reasoning before he will make a move.

(f) Total Intellect

This individual's thought processes rule him. He has little or no feelings for any situation but makes all decisions based on logic. He is a rather cold individual.

With your fingers posed as you see in Diagram "A", notice the palm temperature of your subject. You may notice that his palm is warm, cool, cold or very warm or even hot. While you make a mental note of this temperature sensitivity, notice if his fingers are also the same temperature or different in some way from that of the palm. This is very significant, as you will note later. Test the other hand in the same manner and mentally note the temperature sameness or difference between the palm and tips of the fingers.

Refer once again to Diagram "A" and note the large rectangle with the letters from "A" to "F" and read the description beneath the diagram. You will note that someone with cold fingers and palms will tend to be a "head-led" person in that he does not consult his feelings but does things based more on logic than emotion. He also may be unable to let go of his feelings at an emotional level due to previous traumas resulting in hurt feelings and has resorted to logic to lead him through life. This is the type of person who could push over an old mansion to put up a burger stand if it made sense to him.

The warm-fingered person who has warm palms will be found to be more "heart-led" than "head-led". This is the type of person who would be very upset at seeing an old mansion destroyed to put up a burger stand. This type of person is one who will "leap and then look". You will note that the hand will be warm to very warm and usually the fingers and palm will be uniformly warm. Refer to the letter "A" on the diagram opposite from the letter "F".

Of course, there are many degrees of each type of person and you will be able to discern these through practice. You will sometimes note that the fingers will be cold, or cool, and the palms will be warm. This indicates that this person has a very feeling nature but has been hurt in the past and has learned that he does better if he restricts his feeling nature and observes caution. This type of individual will fall into the "B" category of Diagram "A". You will notice that some people have warmer fingers than palms and this indicates more intellectual control than emotional and will fall into category "E". Some will be evenly balanced between the two, and these will fall into category "C" and "D". This will require practice but you will acquire skill rapidly because it will astonish and amaze you at how accurately you can begin to read someone with just the temperature of the hand to guide you.

With just a few subjects, you will accurately tell clients just what type of person they are and whether they have trouble in letting go of their feelings or if they are totally intellectually oriented and do not consult their feelings.

Touch the person's hand and observe the warmth. Remember that warmth comes from within and reaches outward. Any retraction of love, experiences of fear or rejection or trauma may cause your subject to have pulled back from people in earlier years. This will be reflected in the amount of warmth you feel in the palm and fingers. The cooler the fingers, the greater the holding back of emotion.

Hold both hands and notice if there are any differences between the two. In many readings, I have noticed that one hand was different from the other and have asked about circulatory problems. Most of the differences between hands are caused by improper circulation and your subject may or may not be aware of this type of problem. If you read someone who has had a stroke, you will often notice this difference between his hand temperatures.

Touching of the hands and noticing temperature differences is not psychic; however, it is a springboard for your next technique, which is purely psychic. The touching gets you into harmony and rapport with your clients and lets them know that you are becoming aware of them and their mental and emotional make-up with an excellent degree of accuracy.

Lifeline (Refer to Diagram "B" Figures 1, 2 & 3)

We now enter into the realm of true psychic perception. You have gotten into the proper mental posture and into good harmony with your subjects and are now prepared to give them a reading of their past. It is best if they have told you nothing to this point and that nothing has been asked which would prejudice you in any direction. You must be able to be totally objective and to relate exactly what you see to your subject.

Your mindset is right and now is the time to engage your first effort at mental framing. If you have ever seen a painting made on a black velvet background, then you are way ahead of the game. The first "prop" is to picture a solid black velvet background just like a large backdrop of black velvet. Then picture a white line intersecting the black about in the middle as illustrated in Diagram "B" (figure number two). You will notice that this line will be solid and bright; thin and translucent, be parallel with another line, discolored or you may notice other features about the line. This is your subject's lifeline. To your left is the past, your center is now and to your right represents the future. What we will be concerned with right now is the left area of the line.

When you visualize this picture in your mind and see the line, you must realize that you are creating the mental framework, or prop, and allowing the natural impressions to become visible to you. Thus, the line will represent your subject, and as you practice, you will learn to interpret what you see with an astonishing degree of accuracy. For example, if you see a bright line which seems to be even and consistent from left to right, then you may interpret this as indicating that your subject is operating at his or her maximum capacity, is in good health and is consistently steady in his work or lifestyle. A

DIAGRAM "B"

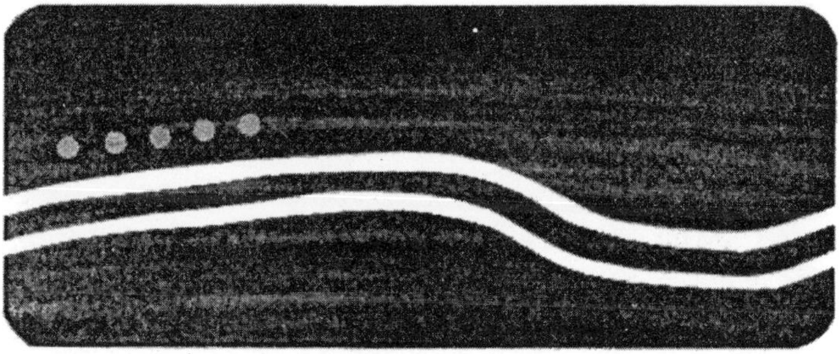

Figure 1

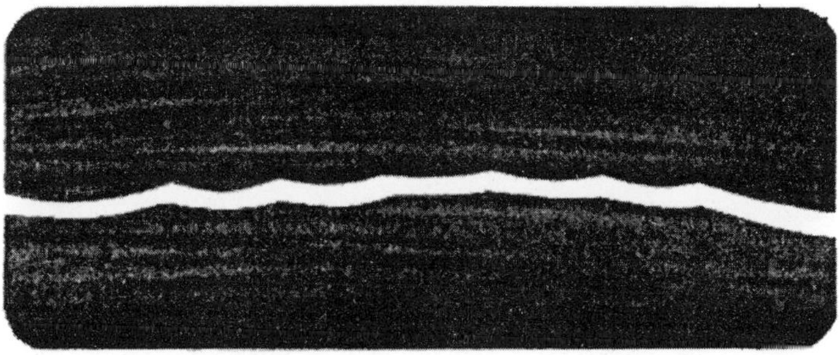

Figure 2

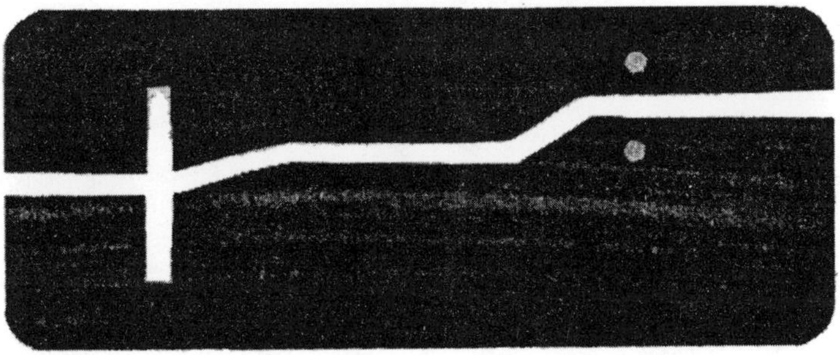

Figure 3

bright lifeline is a good positive indication of his position in life. It indicates happiness and stability with outgoing interests and consistent dependability.

A shallow lifeline, which appears to be somewhat translucent and thin, indicates people who are not operating at their peak efficiency. Something is draining them of energy, and they are not putting forth as much effort into their work or general activities as they otherwise would or could. A thin lifeline is usually the result of past trauma, depression, a problem or unpleasant event which is still in the mind of your subject and which they have not been able to totally release. You will usually see the line bending down somewhere to the left as it moves from left to right. This is somewhat illustrated by figure number one of Diagram "B". This figure, however, shows a brighter line than the one we are describing.

Another type of line is the one noted in figure number two of Diagram "B". This line reflects the type of people who fluctuate in their interests from time to time. You will notice peaks in the line on a somewhat regular basis. This can indicate peaks of excitement or intense activity on weekends with boredom experienced during the week. This will produce an ocean-wave type of line as illustrated. Sometimes you will notice long periods between peaks. This indicates that your subject gets interested in something on occasion but not very often. He may go for long periods without finding anything interesting to do and then gets interested in a hobby. His interest, however, will be short-lived, and the line will rapidly return to the base level and continue level again for some time. When you see this type of line, you are reading an individual who is rather suppressed and cannot sustain an outside interest for any length of time.

Another type of line you will encounter is that of parallel lines. Refer to figure number one of Diagram "B". You will note a lighter line beneath the main line. When you see this type of line, it usually represents a secondary interest such as a second job, strong hobby or some other interest running concurrently with his main interest in life. This type of line will reflect the individual who has other interests in life than working and is maintaining that interest. You may see two, three or four concurrent lines at one time. Usually each line will be of a different intensity, reflecting the degree of interest the individual has in each endeavor. Many times some of the lines will run for a short distance and stop and another will pick up later and continue onward for a while and also stop. This indicates that your subject gets interested in something for a while and then loses interest and goes on to something else.

When reading to the right, or the future, you may notice that one of the underlying parallel lines changes from the bottom and becomes the predominant line. This indicates that something he has been working on at a part-time or secondary basis will become the primary interest in the future.

You will also notice slants in the lifelines.. Notice figure number one of Diagram "B", and you will see a downward slant to the line. This indicates depression, downhill tendencies in a situation, emotional draining events, trauma or other energy-draining events. You can see the line actually drop, and you can notice if the down period is past or still continuing. In figure number one of Diagram "B", the entire picture represents the past so the downtrend is recent but you can see that the subject is starting to come out of the depression.

Another interesting slant is the upward slant. You can notice if your subject is on an uphill swing, indicating that he or she is experiencing an improvement in his life situation. Many times after you have given a reading and indicated your subject's problems to him and discussed with him how he can overcome some of the problems of the past, you will see an immediate uphill elevation of his lifeline. This indicates that he has accepted a mental change of attitude in his life, and you see this in Diagram "B", figure number three. The vertical line represents the present, and the uphill line represents the future. As you can see, the client's future looks upbeat and very positive. The vertical line was inserted to illustrate the present and does not represent an actual line that you will see.

The brightness of the line has been discussed but needs more clarification for greater understanding. Generally the brighter the line, the better the state of affairs with your subject. Brightness of the line indicates bodily harmony and efficient functioning together with a positive attitude overall. Many times I explain to my clients that people operate much like an electric light bulb. If you have a one hundred-watt bulb operating at full brightness, it is also operating at full capacity. If you turn it down to eighty watts, you are operating at less than capacity. Most people can relate to that explanation and understand that they need to do something to get back to full capacity and enjoyment in their life.

One feature which you will notice on many occasions is what I call "flair-ups" in the line. This is not illustrated, but you will be able to see them at times. This indicates extreme emotional upheavals on the part of your subject. Personal conflicts with mates, divorces, business battles and etc., will be reflected in the lifeline as a large expansion of short duration somewhere in the lifeline. This is usually followed by a downward slant of the lifeline as these events produce much energy drain, and time is needed for recovery. I read one lady who had a devastating divorce some five years back, and her lifeline was still in a down state indicating that she had never fully dealt with her problem and had never released it. Once this had been discussed with her and she realized that she truly had never gotten over the divorce, she began to change her lifestyle and recovered completely.

Tinted lines generally represent illness, drugs (legal or illegal), tiredness or other maladies. When I see a lifeline with a yellow tint to it, I generally interpret it as tiredness. If the line is deeper or the color is more pervasive, I usually interpret it as illness. Drug use will show up as yellow in the lifeline as well as irregularities in the lifeline itself. Prescribed medication will usually be indicated by continuous discoloration of light to moderate yellow discoloration.

Dark or "dingy" lifelines are usually severe illness or illness over a long period of time. Sometimes you will see dark discoloration coupled with shallowness and much translucence. You will be able to discern the irregularities in the lines with practice.

When giving a future reading, you will look to your right at the subject's lifeline. You will be able to discern whether or not your subject will have an upswing in life, increased money in the future, meet someone of interest, move to another location, change jobs and many other facets of interest to them. The lifeline will appear the same as when you read to your left, and you will be able to discern ups and downs the same as before. The exception will be that you are reading into the future. Once again, notice figure number three of Diagram "B" and you will see that this subject's line expresses an increase which reflects an upcoming improvement in her lifestyle and position in life.

I do not generally read very far into the future although I can if I want to. I usually read about two or three months ahead. The reason that I hesitate to read far into the future is because most people forget after a short time and cannot relate to events you may say are going to happen years down the road. Most people are interested in their present activity and near future opportunities and upcoming events. However, I have given readings for years in the future with much accuracy. If someone is interested in a long-range reading, then this can certainly be given.

One of the more fascinating aspects of reading lifelines is the ability to see close friends or relatives through your subject. You can read your subject's brother's lifeline, mother, son, daughter or other people who are close to your subject. You can see the line behind the subject's line or off to the side. You will be able to read the second person's line as accurately as the person sitting in front of you.

Many people will come to you and ask about the health or well being of a close loved one, and you will be able to tell them what you see. At times, I have seen those lifelines head downward and cease. I interpret that as an indication of death and will relate this information to the person who has asked about it. However, I repeat, I do not reveal personal death indications to someone I am reading. I feel that this type of revelation would not be in anyone's best interest and could actually become a self-fulfilling prophecy. Your subject could dwell on the matter and bring about his or her own death through an accident or other means because his attention was riveted on the future and he began to think that he had no future to look forward to. This can precipitate many other problems that are not necessary and should be avoided.

CHAPTER 3

HEALTH PICTURE

One of the main concerns of those people who inquire of your reading skills will be their health. Many times they will be healthy themselves but will be very concerned over a relative or friend who has health problems. I wish to state plainly that neither you nor I can play doctor or make any type of pretense or substitution for proper medical help. However, you can take a careful look into the mental image of the physical body and give your observations and interpretations of what you see. What your client does with the information is his own concern.

By now you are in excellent rapport with your subject and have exhibited the appropriate mental posture and employed correct mental framing to arrive at this junction for health determination. Relax with your subject and orient your mind toward physical perceptions and allow your mind to become receptive to subtle impressions that may reflect particular physical conditions.

Your mental frame, or prop, for the health reading is to visualize an outline of a physical body. If you have ever seen an outline of a human body that is used for target practice, this is just what you need to see in your mind. Do not look at your subject but continue looking just off from the subject and picture the outline in your mind. See the outline; and within the outline, see the body as white within the outline. You will then notice different colors imposing upon the white. Black generally means that there have been problems in the area where you see the color black. These are past problems and are not troubling your client at the present time. You may see a black area in or near the heart. Inform your client of what you see, and you will discover that he had a heart attack or some problem dealing with the heart in the past. The black area may be in any portion of the body and may be totally black or faded out slightly, indicating a more remote or distant problem with no current implications.

When you are observing the outline and a red area appears, this is indicative of a current problem and may reflect either a painful situation that your subject knows about or something that is inflamed or irritated that he may not know about. The intensity of the red color indicates the severity of the disturbed area. Light red or pink may indicate slight problems or disturbances that are not so serious.

Scan the entire body picture and make notes of what you see and where the discolored areas are. Red and black may not be the only colors you see. Brown indicates areas of the body that are not functioning properly and are subject to further deterioration and a possible future problem. Note the exact area of the discoloration for your next step.

Once you have noticed an abnormal area, the next process is to imagine that you are looking through a magnifying glass or microscope at the affected area. Magnify the area in your mind and examine what you see. You may see strands that are broken. This may indicate injury to muscle tissue or blood vessels. If you are medically trained, you will be able to recognize and identify the exact organ or describe more completely the affected area and see many shades of colors and many different colors. The main point here is that through proper mental framing and posturing, you can look into someone's body and become aware of things which may be adversely affecting him or her or which may be ready to cause problems in the future. Upon noticing this condition, you may inform your client, and he or she can then visit the doctor for a check-up or verification. Once professional medical experts recognize the problem, your client will be helped by proper treatment.

There was a particular chiropractor that took the course some time back. After using these techniques, he remarked that he could see problems psychically that he could later perform verification tests on, which were totally blind and independent. He said that in each case wherein he performed psychic discernment, the tests confirmed his findings, and his accuracy was nearly 100%.

Practice this technique, and you will develop great insight into upcoming medical problems before they happen and be able to ward off illness ahead of time. At first, you may see a red area and describe a current health problem only to find that your subject has a stomachache from eating too much ice cream. It will take practice to be able to determine the degree of color and intensity of the problem. Once you work at it, you will not be fooled by a transitory stomach ache but can see the true picture and help your subject.

When you hold both hands and begin to notice a temperature difference, you may be picking up on a circulatory imbalance. If you have a subject of this type and arrive at the health reading, you may want to look at this imbalance. You can see it in the form of a red area that may be spread out like a net, indicating blood vessels. Your imagery may be different from mine, but if you use the technique given here you will have the tool necessary for personal development of your own sensitivity methods.

You can do this with people who are close to your subject also. You can see their father, mother, children, husband, wife or others close to them. Read them just as if they were sitting directly in front of you. Remember to look off from your subject. Direct viewing of the subject sometimes is distracting.

Working with the health picture can become very valuable in your everyday life. You can perform regular readings on members of your family or close friends once you get past your own personal ideas or preconceptions and become objective.

There will be many times when your husband or wife will want a health reading. You will be able to spot any upcoming problems and possibly enable him or her to ward off disease before it happens. Of course, this is not to supplant any regular medical check-up or treatment for medical problems.

If you do see a developing problem, magnify the area as best you can, investigate every aspect that you can interpret and then do an overall body scan to include all areas affected by what you have seen. Do not confine your reading to only one specific area of the body because the cause may lie in another part of the body totally unsuspected of being involved in any problems.

Sometimes it is hard to perform the health readings on your loved ones because you will not want to see anything but good health for him or her and will tend to overlook or change your readings to be more favorable than they are.

In today's world, there are so many diseases that are sexually transmitted that having a relationship can be like Russian roulette. Many people who are aware of having a disease will inform any potential mate or partner, but there are those who honestly don't know that they are carrying a deadly virus or other infectious disease until they have infected many other people. As of the writing of this book, more than thirteen million persons worldwide have died of AIDS/HIV virus. It is becoming absolutely imperative that people learn more about their potential sex partner prior to becoming involved in any relationship. What you have learned can now be utilized not only for the protection of the people you are reading but possibly for your personal use as well.

When you take your client's hand and sense the temperature, you will begin your first insight into his or her general health picture. You will notice immediately any variation in the hand temperature and any emotional restraint and sensitivities, as outlined earlier. However, for this course, visualize the body outline as you are holding the hands and form a clear picture of the outline and observe the shaded areas of the body image.

You will remember that the black areas indicate past problems, white areas indicate clarity from disease and the color red or some degree of red indicates on-going or current health problems. When you notice a red area, you are then to focus your attention on that area and expand it in your mind much as you would look at it under a microscope. Enlarge it until you can see the exact spot or organ that is affected. What you will see is similar to an enlargement from a microscope picture.

In areas of the body where there is general infection such as a cold, flu or other respiratory problem, you will notice that the lungs are bright red. In areas of other problems such as kidney problems, you will notice the color red in areas of the kidneys. In other words, a specific infection will show up in specific areas.

Blood infections, such as the AIDS virus, will show up as red throughout the entire body picture or will show up as a red background. I did a reading on a homosexual who had been admitted to a hospital with pneumonia. When performing the reading, I saw the entire background, which is normally velvet black, glowing a bright red. I did not know that he suffered from AIDS at the time, but he shortly died of the virus. Since the reading was done at some distance from where he was hospitalized, I had no way of knowing what his problem was. The AIDS factor was confirmed later, however.

In the event you encounter someone in whom you may or may not be interested, perform a body scan prior to any involvement. You can perform this at a distance and without touching anyone. Touching the hands will give you a lead-in for additional reading, but it can be done without any touch at all. If you see any redness, be certain of the areas of redness that you see and notice if you see the red all over or specifically. If it is seen in a private reading for someone, you will want to mention it to him and let him know what you see. Don't play doctor. Just because you see a red area, you are not qualified to make a medical diagnosis. Just tell your client what you see and let him decide what to do about it, if anything.

If you are reading someone that you may be personally interested in for a possible involvement, you are reading for your own information and protection. It certainly would not be advisable to walk up to someone and inform him that you think he has a disease. The person who suffers at that time might not welcome the information or appreciate the candor.

Use your body scan for self-protection. You certainly don't want to start any relationship with someone who is diseased to begin with. You may want to confirm your reading if you have any doubts in your imagery. You may have occasion to be in the proximity of this individual on other dates and can perform your reading scan again. If you still come up with the same picture, your chances for accuracy are very high, and you should exercise much caution with this person.

If you see totally red in your body image, you must remember that it isn't necessarily AIDS. Cancer can also show up as red either in localized areas or throughout the body, depending upon the type. There again, you will see the red, which indicates a problem. Let the doctor make the diagnosis - not you.

There will be times when you do a body scan when you will notice some black areas but mostly white and translucent imagery. However, you will also notice a negative feeling or heaviness concerning your reading. This may indicate that your subject has a problem, but it hasn't as yet caused any physical manifestations enough to be indicated by discoloration of the body image.

Once you become sensitive to psychic impressions, you also know that you may well hear, feel or sense problems rather than see them in mental imagery. Just because your image is clear, it doesn't mean you are to rush into a relationship yet. Check your inner feelings and general intuition concerning this individual as well as the imagery before making a move.

Another method to utilize is to focus your attention on the body scan but concentrate on the pelvic or below the waist area. You can specifically locate your potential partner's reproductive organs in your image and can observe any discoloration or unusual associated image.

You may well see a clear translucent vaginal impression but may notice a black area nearby. Upon discussion with your subject, she may disclose to you that she had surgery some time back. She may reveal that she has had a hysterectomy or some other corrective measures may have been taken but will have no current problem.

If you are reading someone and notice a discoloration in the pelvic area such as redness, yellow, brown or a dingy tint, you may rest assured that there is some problem that needs attention. It may also indicate a long on-going infection that cannot be cured and also one that you don't want to contract.

I was giving a reading to a man who was interested in a future romantic relationship. As I was reading his future lifeline, I kept noticing a yellow tint on the bottom of the line. Upon further concentration I discerned that he had some type of venereal type of infection and that it had been present for some time. He informed me that he was infected with the Herpes virus and had been suffering from it for several years. He did later marry, but his wife was informed and protective measures were taken for her sake.

I was giving a reading to another young lady when I noticed that she, too, had discoloration in the pelvic area and also was suffering from Herpes. When I informed her of my vision, she acknowledged the infection. She was very upset and worried about any future involvement for fear of being rejected due to her infection. Upon further reading, I informed her that she would meet a gentleman that would understand and who she would be able to form a viable relationship. She met him a few months later and entered into a successful relationship.

One of the most difficult problems to deal with in psychic reading is being emotionally close to the person whom you are reading. Emotional detachment is necessary for accuracy, and this is the one thing that most readers cannot sustain when reading a family member or loved one. Most of us cannot bear to see our mate in anything but good health and anything else is easily blocked out of our consciousness. This renders readings of family or loved ones most difficult.

If you are reading a family member and discover redness or any discoloration other than translucent white,. you may have reason to be alarmed and a check-up may be in order at your doctor's office. This will apply to discoloration in general, and I am not specifically talking about sexual diseases in this case. Learning to be emotionally detached can be very helpful to maintain family health.

When reading someone else through your client, notice another lifeline close to the one you are reading. You may notice that the line is tinted yellow, indicating tiredness, illness or medication including illegal drugs. Yellow seems to cover several relatively mild conditions. However, you may well see redness in the line, weak intensity, inclining or declining. You can read your client's mate, partner or friend as well as if they are right in front of you.

Two of my former students became fast friends. Mary went out of state on business and in the process obtained readings from two psychics. Mary was astounded to receive a reading for Susan from both psychics indicating that Susan was soon to divorce. Both psychics also told her that Susan would remarry, and the psychics called the name of her future husband. Mary learned rather quickly that close friends could indeed be read without having to be present at the time of the reading.

Upon hearing the news that two psychics had predicted her divorce, Susan visited another student friend and asked for a personal reading. He, too, revealed that he saw a wedding in the future for her. Neither person involved in the readings had any prior knowledge that Susan and her husband had already discussed divorce and that it was impending.

By now you can easily see that the view of the psychic can be expanded into virtually an unlimited degree. By focusing on imagery and following up on your intuition, you can discover much information that will not only protect you but your clients as well.

In this consideration, you may well take heed and become aware of possible future problems with your intended. If you look at his or her lifeline as far into the future as you can look and discern honesty, truth, sincerity and loyalty, you may well proceed with your interests. However, if you find any negative indications, discoloration, infidelity or otherwise, you may do well to take a pass. This is why emotional detachment is necessary and if that is not possible, have someone else that you know to be competent do the reading.

CHAPTER 4

PERSONAL RELATIONSHIPS

Separating personal relationships from romantic interests is sometimes difficult. This chapter will confine itself to discussions of personal relationships such as friends, relatives, etc., rather than love relationships involving marriages, dating or romance. Romantic relationships will be covered in a later chapter.

Your proper mind set for this section of your reading is to picture a large wall covered with red velvet flocked wallpaper. The paper can have pretty designs on it if you so desire, but use the same picture each time you perform your readings. Picture the wall uniformly red except for the center of the wall. Imagine that in the center of the wall a picture has been removed and has left a lighter area than the surrounding wall. I like to see a pretty red wall and a slightly yellow oval space in the center. This oval space represents your subject's heart (emotional - not physical).

Surrounding this light area you will see faces of people who are close to your subject. Notice the location in the image of where each face is and describe it to your subject. If you see a young girl just below the level of the light area and looking toward that area, you might say, "I see a young girl looking toward you. She feels much love for you, and your relationship with her is good. She looks to you, and there is much trust." Additionally, you may go on and describe this girl's hair color, facial expressions, color of eyes, etc. On the other hand, you may notice someone who is looking away from your subject. This may be expressed as, "I see a young man with very dark hair who is looking away from you. I feel that this man is seeking his own direction and is somewhat resisting you or your efforts toward him. I do see, however, that there is some looking back, which indicates that he still cares for you and there is some concern for you, but he is trying to move in a new or different direction." Your interpretation and expression may be different from mine, but the truth of the matter will still be expressed.

You must bear in mind that when you are giving a personal relationship reading, your subject will already know much of what you are telling him. Don't hedge on your reading or try to tell your subject what you think he will enjoy hearing. Your subject will immediately know that you are not being honest with him, and your credibility as a reader will suffer irreparable damage. You must be accurate and describe what you see - good or bad. If you see disturbances between your subject and someone he loves or is close to, then tell him! If you are to be a professional, you must handle your readings as a professional.

Many times when you employ this mental frame, you will encounter no images. You may be tempted to put images where there are no images. However, if you will simply reveal that you see no one person close to your client at this time, your reading will be exactly accurate. Your client will reveal that he truly is lonely and needs to seek companionship. Be true to yourself during your readings, and your skill and accuracy will astound you as well as your clients. Remember to separate your wishes and desires from what you are seeing for someone else. Your job is to interpret and report what you see and not to change it to suit yourself.

Many times you will read for someone who wants to know about his son or daughter. When you arrive at this point in your readings, you may then take a look at his lifeline, closeness to your client, inclinations in the future and other pertinent issues. Also, you may note any changes in the closeness to your client of a child, friend or relative.

If you sense that the offspring is having trouble in his direction of life, you may advise your client and make him aware that he needs to seek additional help or give more guidance to that person in order to help him.

When you see a face on the wall, notice the eyes and the direction he is looking. Notice if there is a bi-directional viewpoint. This is to say that the image may be looking toward your client and looking away at the same time. This could indicate that the client's offspring is simply seeking his own life or it could indicate animosity against your client. You will be able to discern the difference as you become more adept at your readings. This can usually be noted by observing the facial expressions of the images you observe. Notice also the image's lifeline color. Is it clear and bright or tinted with yellow? Is it straight or does it shift directions frequently, indicating inability to find his way? Observe as clearly as you can all of the detail you can become aware of. You may notice the style of clothing in your image, and it may indicate an attitude your subject has which may be reflective of some type of symbolic situation. If you fail to see an image, you may rest assured that this person doesn't feel close to the people he is asking you about, and you won't be able to provide any information for him. You can't read what isn't there. If you see nothing, admit that you can't see anything and move on. You can't fake information on someone of whom you know nothing and with whom your subject is very familiar. Tell what you see and nothing more.

As you begin your readings, you will notice that you will run into images that are very clear and yet do not describe anyone when your client seems to know. When this happens, ask your client to look back in time, and you will find that the image was of someone who was very close or influential in the life of your client. It may have been a schoolteacher, grandfather or friend he had at an early age and, subconsciously, has never forgotten. Many times you will describe a mother's child at age four or five only to find that this "child" is now thirty years old, but the mother still thinks of him as being only about five because she was so emotionally close to him at that time in his life. You must always remember that you are reading your client's subconscious and not the conscious mind. Mind reading refers to being able to read someone's Beta brain wave pattern, not the Alpha. What you are reading is psychically contained within the Alpha pattern and is not "mind reading".

On many occasions, I have been asked to describe any person that I may see in the future for my client. Take a look at your client's lifeline to your right and observe pictures or faces that may come into close proximity. Describe the image to your client and relate to him the time frame within which you expect that he will meet this new person. Time and again you will be called and informed that your client has just met the person whom you described some months back for them.

Usually when your client asks for this type of information, it concerns romance or future romantic involvement. This will be covered in more detail in the section dealing with the subject of romance. Sometimes, however, you will describe a new boss, new friend or someone who will come into your client's life that will be important to him in ways other than romance.

CHAPTER 5

SPIRITUAL AWARENESS

Your clients who come in for readings will include agnostics, atheists, religious zealots and people from all walks of life. Most are warm-hearted people who are seeking counsel or guidance. The method by which you will know just how spiritually inclined your subject is will now be made clear to you.

When you perform your lifeline readings of the past, look just above the line and you will notice points of light that I prefer to call "Sparkles". These points of light represent your client's prayer life, meditation, inner introspection or his degree of interest and participation in communing with his higher aspirations. You will be able to tell how much of this spiritual inner contact he has been doing either now, in the past, or how much he will be doing in the future.

Refer to Diagram "B", figure number one, and you will notice that the points of light proceed for a while and then stop. This subject had a stable faith as a child, but, as she matured, she became distracted by the material events of our everyday world. She "forgot" her spiritual heritage.

When she was told that she did have at one time a very

close relationship with her faith, she admitted that she could pray and feel very good afterward but had not done so in many years. She then decided to return to her early upbringing and immediately began to feel better, and new doors were opened for her.

Many people are raised in various denominational faiths and do establish certain habits as children or young adults, which strengthen their inner confidence. When they get away from these strengthening processes, many of them feel "lost". After a reading, many clients will return to their established faith and find a renewal of strength and inner confidence. It has been my finding that many people who lose sight of their faith do tend to become like ships without a rudder and may well become lost in a "sea of distractions".

Another factor you can observe in the area of spiritual awareness is that you can read the number of sparkles available to an individual. My interpretation of these "sparkles" is that they are angels and available to help your clients for the asking. If you will notice Diagram "C", figure number one, you will notice that I have drawn points above the head. These are the points of light you will see above your client's head. I generally see from one to five, and the color varies from brilliant white to blue, and I have seen some red ones. It is my feeling that the white ones are "primary angels", and the blue ones are "secondary angels". I have just recently discovered that the red ones sometimes indicate on-going illness.

Your interpretation of the points of light may differ from mine, but I have to express to you what I feel in order that you may research the matter for yourself. I feel that the angels are present and will not interfere with your client's life but will only help if asked through meditation or prayer or inner communion of your client's choice. Through various techniques utilized by different individuals, these points of light, or angels, will provide guidance or intuitive directions for your client. Some people refer to them as "guides". I realize that this may well be conjecturing on my part but I can see them and do get the feeling that what I have described is accurate. You may have different interpretations than mine and spiritual impressions may take on a different meaning with you than with me. However, I stand with my impressions until someone shows me a better way or better interpretation.

Once I have gotten into a spiritual reading situation and have established the accuracy with my client, I then counsel him on greater spiritual awareness for his personal life improvement. Many times I have seen clients change their spiritual consciousness, and their lifeline has brightened up considerably with an

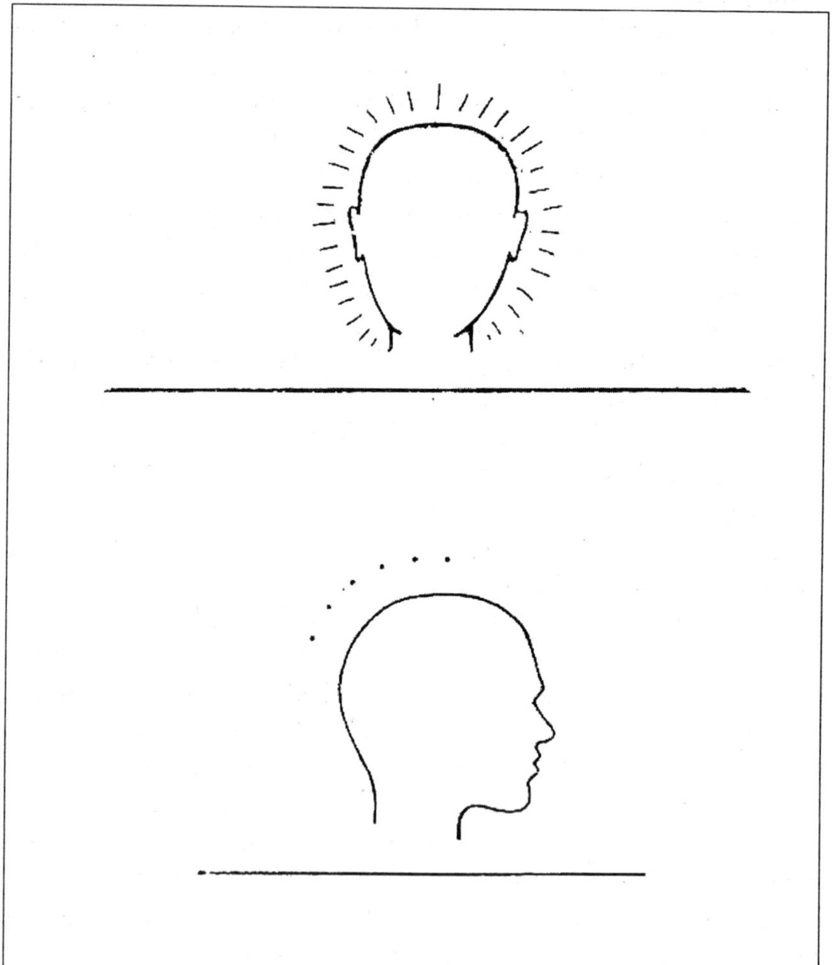

immediate upswing noted in their future reading. Remember that your client can change his or her future by changing the way he thinks and so can we. We are all governed by how we think and if we find some new understanding of ourselves, we can soar beyond our former dreams.

There have been many occasions when I saw absolutely no spiritual inclination whatsoever in the lifeline of my subject. There are some people who are not seeking spiritual interests but consider the world to be only what they can see and prove scientifically. At least, this is what they think on the conscious level. When dealing with this type of people, you will often find that they are challenging you rather than seeking help or advice. When you give them a reading and are accurate, they have to admit to a "sixth sense" type of experience. For them to admit something beyond what they personally can prove is to begin to open their mind to the greater reality of life and to begin to understand that there is much more than what we realize or can prove on an objective level. Often I have read skeptics only to have them become avid and devout students. Once they have been convinced, they realize that much can be opened up for them.

In summation, you can determine to what degree your client has been engaging in spiritual interests in the past, is now, and will be in the future. You can even enhance his spiritual awareness through pointing out methods and techniques whereby he can become receptive to inner perceptions and intuitive impulses that he had always ignored in the past.

I do not attempt to make converts of anyone or to push religion on anyone. However, I can recommend that my client seek out an outlet for spiritual direction that will uplift him and reinforce his spiritual growth. I encourage him to become active in the faith or belief of his choice and to pursue spiritual avenues in life rather than purely material. Your sincere interest in your client will assist him to gain greater insight into the true meaning of life and enter into a greater understanding with his own inner awareness as a person as well as with his fellow man.

CHAPTER 6

FINANCES

One of the main concerns you will discover when reading for people is that they are extremely concerned about their finances. Jobs, money and financial security are high priorities with many of your clients, and your ability to see their financial picture is a must in order to give an overall view of their life.

When you have read this far and have dealt with as much material as we have already covered, reading your client's financial picture will be just a continuation of what you are already doing. You will shift your mental posture from one of concern about personal and spiritual things to money. When doing this, you will find that your reading becomes easier because it is easier to feel objective about finances than it is to deal with someone's personal life or relationships or emotional connections. Finances will actually give you a "breather" before you have to get back into the romantic interests which will follow the financial picture.

When looking for money in the lifeline of the subject, focus your attention on the color green and observe this coloration along the lifeline from past, present and into the future. You will notice an even parallel or possibly a green-tinted line. You may not notice anything until you come to an elevation in the lifeline and then at the base of the line, you will notice a ball of green. This will signify that an increase of money was at the core of your client's upswing in the lifeline. You may notice that there is no change that you can discern and that you do not feel that there will be any change in your client's financial picture. If you care to view the distant future, you may see changes further on down the line.

Your view of money changes will sometimes be negative. You will see a decline of finances reflected in diminishing green or abrupt halts in the green color accompanying the lifeline. This may be in job terminations, loss of money on an investment or any number of things. Just the reverse is true if you see a sudden influx of money in someone's life. Don't hesitate to tell someone if you see a sudden influx of money simply because you personally don't understand where it may come from. Many times the subject will not understand where it may come from either. On many occasions, your clients may receive gifts, inheritances, windfalls, etc. Report just what you see, and let the chips fall where they may.

In Diagram "B", figure number three, you will notice a "stepping stone" increase in this client's lifeline. If you looked at the base of the increase and saw a ball of green, you can easily know that this individual will have an increase of salary and a promotion in his or her job and that future looks bright for him with greater prosperity and more opportunities. You can see promotions in his job status without a corresponding salary increase as in changes of responsibility, moving into a different department or other facets of work with upward movement, but not necessarily having changes in monetary income.

When your mind posture is in the money mode, you will be tuned into money matters rather than other events, and you will essentially give the same type or style of reading as previously but with new emphasis. You will be actually reading the same lifeline but with a different viewpoint. You can read the same line several times and all with entirely different emphasis. What you skillfully look for in a lifeline is what you will be able to obtain from it.

The lessons that you learn in this course are but tools for further advancement. You will be able to reach vastly greater distances into a life as you practice and learn what to look for. There is nothing that a human being has ever done that can't be seen by someone if he cares to look and has the ability and training to do so.

When you are asked to comment on your client's stock investments, you will be confronted with conflicting options. There will be your client's emotional feelings concerning the investment that he or she has already made and, on the other hand, what you objectively perceive from the stock that you tune into.

Stocks or bonds represent companies, and companies represent people who have put energy and work into building and guiding the company. What you will look for are impressions of moving ahead or holding back. When you feel heaviness about an investment, you may well want to look at the line of the stock or investment. You may see the lifeline of the investment very much as you would read a person individually. You will see the line move up or down or it may remain steady. If you see any black forces underneath or near the stock or other investment, avoid it altogether! What you will pick up in this matter may well be greed or avarice on the part of someone within the company who has some control of the financial situation or is planning something which is not in the best interest of the investors.

A young man who wanted to invest in a venture that would involve his future in politics approached me. I saw an image of the person who was asking him to make an investment. I also saw black undertones associated with that person, and I recommended that he take a closer look before leaping into the transaction. When I said this, the young man revealed that he was aware of his potential partner's past indiscretions but felt that this was past and that he could trust the man now. However, he did take a pass on the investment, and he later found that it was a wise decision.

Many clients will approach you and ask which direction they should go concerning investment decisions. They may have many decisions or choices and can't seem to decide which choice they need to make or which will be of most benefit in the future.

When reading for selection of choices, you will notice spurs from the original lifelines in the future. You may see several spurs coming out from the line, and some of them will be short and others will have a longer life. The spurs indicate sideline interests and can concern investment or other activities. Note the number of spurs, the intensity of brightness and the duration of the spur. The way I do this is by numbering the spurs as choice number one, two, three, etc. The brightest spur is generally the one that he will follow, or at least should follow. I may see spur number one, two and three and notice that spur number three is the brightest and longest. I will then inform my client that I see him taking the third choice in a given matter. You don't have to know just what the matter is but you will be able to tell your client which choice he will probably make. After your reading, your client is free to choose any of his or her interests and totally cancel out your prediction. We are all free to choose. However, you will find that he invariably chooses that which you have seen and find that it was the right and most prosperous decision to make at that time.

When you read spurs off from the main lifeline, they can also apply to hobbies, miscellaneous interests of short-term duration or sampling new work interests and many other areas of everyday life. When you are in tune with money, however, you will pick up monetary interests rather than general interest topics.

Making financial choices can also apply to investing in real estate, art, diamonds or other items as well as stocks and bonds. Through proper sensitivity you can develop a feeling for investments that will be good for your clients. When giving your financial reading, you must also consider emotional perceptions involving your client's orientation and mindset. You will be able to tune in on the investments that best suit them on a personal basis. Give them your opinion, and they can make their own decision after they leave your office.

When reading investment items, you will find that you don't have a close connection to go on. Since your client doesn't know anything about the people who control the company, you may misread the investment and think that what you are getting is from the investment but, in fact, is coming from the subconscious of your client. His or her feelings concerning the matter may be totally erroneous and lead the client to financial disaster. If you cannot disassociate from your client and tune in on the investment and know that you are doing so, it is better to avoid financial readings altogether. This requires a totally different mental posture and mind frame. Keep to your area of expertise until you have mastered each step one at a time. Skill comes with seasoning of practice. Once you know the difference, however, you can greatly help many people secure a sound investment and plan for a promising future.

When interpreting spur lines, you will notice that one line will tend to predominate over the others. In some cases, it will come from a small spur and build into a parallel line beneath the main line and then come from the bottom to the top and become the predominate line. You will sometimes notice this when you perceive that your client is planning to go into his or her own business. The secondary line you read was an interest that your client had been working on, and it gradually became, or will become, a primary force in his life. You will find that this happens quite a bit with sales people or highly motivated people who want to work for themselves rather than someone else. You can actually see when the transfer from employee to employer takes place.

When you are called in to give an entire company a reading, you will first want to read all of the powerful and influential people who govern the company a personal reading. Then you can form a composite vision of what can be expected from the company in terms of future expectations. If you see many problems in the lives of the chief executives, you can rest assured that the company will also experience turmoil and trouble. After all, a company is only made up of people, and people tend to project their personalities into the success or failure of what they create in the form of companies or any other venture. You cannot expect a convicted repeat safe cracker to be a trustworthy bank president. Likewise, an upright individual would have no subconscious darkness that would lead him or her into theft or fraud and would endeavor to make the company succeed. Be careful in your reading because you have to look for the darkness and ill intent of your client. Be certain that you read for undercurrents, shadows or subterfuge that would undermine the success of the company.

In my more than twenty years of investigative work involving forensic hypnosis, pre-employment screening and interrogation, I have seen much of the dark side of man. I look for this when queried about business dealings and financial ventures with people with whom my client has no working knowledge. I have seen black areas in people's lifelines. This indicates that wrongdoing is afoot and that this individual was not trustworthy or honest in his business dealings. If you see this type of image, consider it a warning and temper your reading accordingly. Dishonest dealings can be seen as well as anything else.

There was a man whom the police brought in on one occasion accused of stealing merchandise from a truck. I was asked to administer truth verification testing procedures (nothing to do with psychic reading) and advise them of my opinion. While performing the testing, I noticed an image of the man behind the truck removing merchandise. After performing the test, areas of deception were noted. He confessed that he, indeed, had participated in the theft from the truck. Do not accuse anyone of wrongdoing based on your psychic perceptions. You can misinterpret your impressions or misconstrue the entire situation and get yourself into quite a precarious position. Simply note your impressions and adjust your reading accordingly. Make mental notes of honesty, openness, trustworthiness and other character traits and move ahead cautiously.

You can also detect deception in normal reading circumstances. I was once listening to a man who was making statements concerning his alcoholic problem. He was starting to talk about his conviction that he would never drink again when I saw blackness near his head. I immediately realized that he was telling a lie, and within one week my vision had proven correct.

There was an interesting occasion when I was listening to a man discuss memory techniques in the local church. During his discussion, I was much impressed with the tremendous ability that he displayed in being able to remember the entire Bible and his methods for teaching the children to memorize scripture. However, after a while, I noticed that I had a mental image of a large white area on top of a small white area. I felt that the image indicated that this person was trying to fit his intellectual knowledge into his faith structure but was not able to do so. He had a lot of head knowledge, but his ability to believe what he knew wasn't keeping pace. There weren't any indications of blackness or deception on his part. However, he later indicated that he had experienced some difficulties in his life with his marriage and other personal problems which clearly indicated that the image I had seen was correct. In all of this man's sincerity, he was not able to have total faith in what he was saying.

Remember when dealing with financial matters, you will more often come up with the emotion of greed and selfishness than you otherwise would in a normal reading. Outright wrongdoing will also be evident in your mental images so be careful and think about what you are going to say before informing your client of your impressions.

If you are planning to invest any money in stocks, bonds, etc., gather all of the information you can about the company including the Chairman of the Board, President or man or men who direct the operation. Calmly relax and peruse the materials before you with an open and non-prejudicial state of mind. See what feelings or impressions you receive from each company or portfolio before you. Choose the one that gives you the greatest degree of a positive feeling and assurance or general feeling of abundance. It is best to cover up the materials and arrange them in such a fashion that you will not consciously know which company or investment will be your best potential from your logical reasoning mind. Sense which will afford a greater return and go with your feelings.

Visualize your lifeline some time into the future, and then picture a green line alongside the lifeline. Know that this green image represents your finances and see which direction the line moves when you are considering one of the investment profiles. If the line moves upward on one more than the others, the indication is that your return will be greater with that particular investment than the others.

When you perform this procedure with your friends or clients, it may be easier because you have no vested interest in the project. I sometimes find it difficult to remove my own interest from the readings, and thus I prefer to ask someone else to do a financial reading for me to confirm that what I have seen is actually factual. In financial matters, it is far too easy to let your imagination run away with you and give you false readings.

These procedures and techniques for financial gain would fill an entire volume. I am only giving you the basics here, and you can expand on your own initiative and make experiments to determine which way benefits you to the greatest extent possible.

I would recommend that you start with small investments and give it enough time to determine which way and to how much degree of superiority one investment would have had over another before you make any serious commitment.

CHAPTER 7

ROMANCES

One of the most important concerns of the vast majority of your clients will involve their romantic interests in life. You will be asked what your impressions are of their present love affiliations, future prospects for marriage or relationships, or what can be done concerning present problems with a mate or loved one. Many times the entire reading will revolve around this area of their life. For this type of reading, you will need the mental framework of the wall with the flocked velvet wallpaper and the light oval area in the center of the wall and the mind posturing for personal or other romantic situations. Some of these situations will be good and some will be not so good, and even bad in some cases. Tune your mind into becoming receptive to love, closeness and extreme emotions of all descriptions. However, you must remain as objective as possible, or you may find yourself getting personally involved in your own emotional feelings and rendering your reading a personal counseling session rather than trying to relate what you see from an observer's perspective. Your client's situation may have a tendency to bring you to tears, and you may well develop so much empathy for him that you lose all pretenses at objectivity. However, with practice, you will be able to keep your feet on the ground and deliver not only a good reading but also excellent advice as to how your client may overcome his or her personal problem at hand.

Clear your mind from all past influences, readings, images or any past discussion. Picture the wall anew with a clear slate and begin tuning in to the central oval area. If you see an image in dead center of the oval in your mental picture, then the mate of the individual you are reading is fulfilling his or her needs and is totally in his or her heart, and there is no room for anyone else or anything else. However, that situation tends to be more idealistic than reality and rarely will you find the oval completely filled. In most cases, you will find that the image of the person you see will fill only a portion of the oval. This indicates that the mate is supplying only a portion of the client's needs, and there is some emptiness in the life of your client. You can tell how much of a void there is by noticing how much space is not filled up by the image of the mate.

Now observe which way the image is looking. If the image of your client's mate is looking straight at the center of the oval, then your client's mate is totally committed to him and has no other interest outside of their relationship. If, however, the image shows the man or woman looking toward your client's oval area but also seems to look in another direction, then you have a divided interest with some deep feeling toward his or her mate but also some self-interest in another direction.

A split image may indicate interest in another person, new job interest, ego difficulties or other personal problems that may or may not be interfering with your client's mate's ability to devote total commitment in the marriage or relationship. One of the reasons may or may not necessarily be that each person is not loving and totally committed to each other but that they are just not matched psychologically to each other to the degree necessary for total mutual fulfillment. You can discern all of this from the image that you see closest to the your client's oval area on the velvet wall.

When you see the image of your client's mate looking downward and the image itself is slightly below that of the mate, you are seeing that your client's mate feels less worthy than his or her spouse. You are seeing how much regard he has for his mate. If the image is slightly above your client, then you are seeing a mate who looks "down" on his or her spouse. This may be a condescending attitude which you can pick up through the image or other attitudes or superiority conflict.

Many readings will show that most partners are not totally fulfilled with each other, and you will see varying degrees of intensity of emotion connected with these images, and you will be able to describe your clients' relationships quite accurately with their close loved ones.

At times you will see someone who has no one in the oval area. This indicates that there is no person in whom he is experiencing emotional or love fulfillment at this point in time. Even though he may be married or has been involved in a relationship for some time, there is still no fulfillment within his heart. There will be a void in his life and you will be able to pick up on this and discuss it with him.

When you are asked about personal romantic relationships, you will often pick up an image of someone with whom the client was involved some time in the past. This is because he has never released that particular individual from his heart. Remember what you are reading is not the conscious mind, but the subconscious mind. A former marriage partner may well have had such an impact on your client's emotions that he will never be able to completely release this person from his life. You will note this more if the relationship was one of true love and ended in death or emotions other than animosity.

Many of your images will be those of someone who is completely outside of any romantic relationship. You may pick up on an older person in whom your client had deep trust and loved very much. That individual will still tend to be in the heart or subconscious of the individual you are reading.

Many times I have described the image I saw only for the client to tell me that he didn't know anyone of that description. After a few minutes more, he recognized someone whom he had known many years prior when growing up. He remarked that he had experienced a great closeness with this individual and much trust.

In a case like this, his romantic interests are somewhat blocked by old attachments and emotional holdbacks to the past. This is especially true in the area of previous marriages or earlier close relationships. Heart-led people are the most vulnerable to this type of emotional blockage. Sometimes the hold to the past is so strong that your client can have no present relationship of any lasting value.

Releasing old holds is never easy for anyone. It becomes harder when the feelings are suppressed and denied by the conscious mind but very alive on the subconscious level. Your client may give many reasons why his present love is wonderful and great, but he just can't understand why his feeling isn't deep enough to sustain a good relationship. You will be able to clearly see why your client is having problems and be able to explain it to him and help him to deal with the reality of the situation and clarify it. Many times, just having someone point out the truth to the client will start the ball rolling toward recovery and release from the past.

When you see the images, describe the facial features, hair color and any other characteristics that you can to clarify just who this person is. When giving a past reading and observing your client's lifeline, you will often observe flares in the line indicating emotional upset, and it will often be related to the past emotional holds we have just discussed. At times you will be able to describe the exact individual who was involved in the flair-up in the past and explain just what problem your client is having in dealing with this trauma.

At times, you may see more than one image in a romantic relationship. I saw one girl who was dating two young men and couldn't decide which one she wanted to marry. One was well-suited for her and gave her an uplifted feeling and was supportive. The other browbeat her and treated her in a negative way. She knew that he wasn't good for her but she couldn't turn him loose. When it was explained to her that she was holding on to him to punish herself, she then understood that she had experienced an incident in the past wherein feelings of guilt were involved. She then understood why she was holding onto him and made her decision accordingly.

Another lady asked about marriage in her future. I saw a beautiful wedding dress and a formal event within three months and related this to her. She informed me that the description of the dress was exactly like the one she had already purchased and that indeed a wedding was planned for three months from the date of the reading. She had withheld information from me to test if I truly could read her with any degree of accuracy.

When you begin observing romantic interest images, you will be able to tell exactly how much love is present from one person to another. You can tell by looking at the image and observing which way the eyes are looking, the underlying flow of emotion toward the oval area, the countenance of the facial picture of the image you are reading and many other indicators which will reveal to you the information. You will be able to determine subterfuge in the relationship, honesty, loyalty and many other traits. This is why you must disconnect your emotions from that of your client. You must be as objective as possible while still maintaining as much empathy as you can allow yourself without interfering with your reading.

In the event that your client wants to ascertain any romantic involvement in the future, your procedure is to observe the future lifeline and open your mind for images of people coming into close proximity. You may observe that in about two months a man will enter your client's life and sphere of activity. You will be able to describe this man to her and tell her how close the relationship will be and how long it will last. You can read his lifeline through her future lifeline and tell the type of temperament he has. You can give her a health reading of her future potential mate and many other factors as you go along. You must bear in mind that we all have freedom of choice and she can totally reject or disregard your predictions and change her future for her own interest, and your reading will not manifest as you see it.

There was a man I knew who was having marital difficulties. He consulted several psychics and obtained a consistent reading from each one. All of them said that his marriage was through and that it was no use going on. He decided differently, and he and his wife were reconciled and are still married to this day. We can all change our lives and are not bound to anyone's predictions. Had he not made an effort at reconciliation, he, undoubtedly, would have divorced his wife long ago. However, if your client doesn't make changes to avoid your predictions, then you may rest assured that your accuracy will be better than 80% and much higher in most cases. There are times when you can foresee that a mental attitude change will be made. I have seen this many times when doing readings on sincere and cooperative clients.

The emotional intensity of the future relationship can be noted in the brightness of the lifeline of your client. Naturally, the brighter the line, the greater will be the intensity of the relationship, and the opposite is also true. You may notice the intensity of both lines and determine if the relationship will be balanced. Whatever you see, report it accurately and honestly. Don't try to paint "rose gardens" and make things appear better than they are or better than they will be.

I've known readers who couldn't bear to tell their clients anything but good news. Their clients left anticipating miraculous things, and when they didn't materialize as predicted, they were bitterly disappointed and upset with their reader. You must present your reading in an unbiased and truthful manner in order to gain credibility. Life is never totally happy or totally unhappy, and if you try to make it so, you will be attempting to manipulate your client's life to your expectations rather than what will actually be experienced. Be honest. It will be appreciated and result in establishing a good reputation for you.

When dealing with romantic readings, you will come across some people who want involvements but, nevertheless, block out close relationships because of deep fears of rejection or hurt. They will tell you that they desperately want to have someone to love, but you will be able to discern otherwise. They may have been hurt earlier in life and still nurture the hurt in their subconscious. This type of person will find ways to kill a prospective suitor's interest early in the relationship. He won't know consciously why his relationships don't work out, but you will be able to detect this and bring it to his conscious awareness.

Many times you will be able to determine that the lack of fulfillment is only caused by temporary business or other personal interference and not because of other romantic interests. However, if you see another face at the end of your partner's gaze, you may have cause to wonder.

One of my students had a reading by a fellow student, and a second woman was clearly indicated in the reading. The student then revealed that he had been having an affair for some years and had never told anyone about it before. You can read your mate's true interest if you can remain emotionally detached long enough to be totally objective.

The technique for discernment of romantic interests is the oval picture method described earlier. Picture your mate or partner and carefully observe where your personal image is within his or her oval frame area. If your picture is totally within the frame, you may rest assured that you are totally fulfilling his or her emotional needs. If, however, your picture is only partly contained within his or her oval frame area, then you may well not be fulfilling enough of your partner's needs.

Once you have made the determination of the degree of emotional fulfillment, notice your own oval frame of reference. Once you have imagined the picture frame and know that it is your own, then look to see if your mate's image is totally within the confines of the frame in your own image or is only partially contained within the frame. You will then discover how much of your own needs are being met by your partner. Once you have made this determination, you may then go on to determine if your mate has any outside interests. To do this, you must observe your image of your partner and see which direction he or she is facing. If he is facing toward the center of your personal image, then you can reasonably feel that he is interested in only you and has no other romantic interests. However, if he is looking toward you but also in another direction, you can have reasonable suspicion that he has another interest. Follow the direction of his gaze far enough, and you will see what he is interested in. Many times my students have done this with their own mate only to discover that the interest was in a business venture which was taking much thought on the part of the mate or partner they were reading.

If you want to pursue this further and continue to explore the imagery, you may move forward on his or her lifeline and discern meetings and liaisons between your partner and the image you have just seen. Again, it may only be a friend or something other than romance or actual sex. However, as you move along the lifeline, carefully monitor your inner guiding feelings, which will be associated with the imagery. You will be able to discern the magnetic attraction, if indeed the involvement is romantic. However, if you sense no negativity, deceit, darkness or any other perception which would indicate that your partner is cheating on you, then do not make that disastrous postulation. Remember that most psychics are not 100% correct, and you may well misinterpret your imagery or your feelings or both.

Misinterpretation on your part may be due to close emotional involvement. Jealousy will make your readings totally inaccurate, and your imagery will be of your own making to support your insecurity and will have no relation whatsoever to a true psychic picture. If you cannot detach yourself from this situation, it is better to engage the services of a professional psychic. Many times you will need to visit two or three to gain a more accurate picture which is totally unbiased.

A lady visited me and requested that I give a reading on her husband. I looked at both lifelines and discerned that he was involved with other people but that no romantic interest was present. However, she didn't believe me and engaged the services of a private detective to prove to herself that he was running around on her. She came back for another reading and brought pictures with her indicating that he was indeed in the presence of other people. However, even the detective couldn't prove any misconduct on her husband's part. She still didn't believe either the detective or me.

Another lady obtained a reading under the pretense of being interested in finances. However, when I formed the oval frame, I noticed that there was no one there. I mentioned to her that I thought that she was lonely, but I did see a man nearby looking toward her but also looking in another direction. I also felt that was tension between her and this man. She stated that her husband has been running around on her and that she and he had been having many marital difficulties. He was still interested in her but wasn't fulfilling any of her needs.

You must also remember that you can read your client's close associates, family members or friends at the same time you are reading your client. You may well be reading a lady when you see her husband's lifeline. You can then discern any physical problems, infections, diseases or other abnormalities and relate this information to your client.

There will be times when you describe people coming into your client's life, and there will be no particular reason or emotional involvement of any kind whatsoever. I recently gave a lady a reading and described a gentleman that she would soon meet. He was very handsome, had brown hair which was dark and full. His face was described clearly as well as the type of clothing he would be wearing when she met him. The lady did meet this man when she went to a college alumni function. He was the first person she met, and he was very friendly with her and they talked a lot at the meeting. She never saw him again, and no romance developed from the meeting.

Your job is to tell what you see and exactly how you see it. Do not make inferences or personal preferences in your comments about the people you see. I was careful not to lead her on in expectations that something more than a meeting would occur because I didn't receive any impressions either way from the reading.

CHAPTER 8

COUNSEL AND ADVICE

When you give readings to various clients, you will invariably run into people who need your counsel. They will seek advice on what to do concerning various matters that you may bring up in the reading. You may foresee tremendous changes for your client or see that there will be no change at all for the foreseeable future.

The manner in which you may advise your client will rest with your interpretation of his composite imagery. You will take into consideration the past lifeline and circumstances, the health consideration and the future lifeline impressions. The discussion you may have with your client can change his future lifeline considerably. I have given readings to people with the future lifeline showing certain patterns, and new decisions were made after discussing their problems and enlightening them to a greater understanding. The changes reflected immediately in the future lifeline readings.

There was one lady for whom I could see no future lifeline. There was nothing but a "wall of darkness" every time I tried to see into her future and read her line. Her past had been riddled with depression and emotional upset. We stopped and discussed her past and in so doing, she realized that she had been anticipating death and, indeed, would have welcomed it as a method of relief. When she realized this, she was able to emotionally release the blockage from severe rejection originating from a former marriage. She then began to be able to have a new outlook. When I then tried to read her future line, it was bright and clear.

In this client's past, I had observed that as a little girl, she had been very religious and it showed with many sparkles for several years. However, she got involved with an unsavory character and became totally distracted from her faith. When she realized this, she returned to her familiar upbringing and a hopeful note was struck within her subconscious mind. The more we talked, the better she felt; and by the end of the reading, she had taken on a totally new outlook that later resulted in the clearing of the blockage to her future. A later reading revealed that the darkness had dissipated, and her line showed stepping stones of improvement and new hope for her future.

You can see from the above example that you can be of invaluable help to people in need through being able to see into their problem from an objective point of view. You can enable them to see the right direction. On many occasions, I strongly recommend that my client retreat to a favorite place of beauty or quiet until he can unite his head and heart and re-establish communication with his inner self. Sometimes it takes five minutes, five hours or it may take five days. I suggest to him that he take whatever time is necessary in order to re-establish his priorities and achieve a realization of "oneness" within himself. If he is religious, I recommend prayer; if not, then meditation or whatever he can relate to.

If your client follows your advice, it will open up avenues of personal improvement that will give him tremendously uplifting possibilities, and you will have helped a struggling soul on the journey through life.

Many clients already know what to do but need someone

else to agree with them and understand their plight. I have counseled many ladies and gentlemen as well who knew that a change was needed in a romantic situation but couldn't do it alone. After the reading many of their problems became amply clear, and they were able to seek professional help and make up their own mind with clarity and certainty of purpose.

There was one gentleman who had problems with his son who was on drugs. During the reading, he inquired about his son, and the lifeline of the boy was tinted yellow and seemed to vary considerably with many ups and downs. I stated to him that it appeared that his son had lost his way and was suffering from some type of medication or drug effects.

When the information was revealed to my client, he blurted out that he had been "coddling" him in an effort to try to dissuade him from drug use. Upon realizing his own pent-up anger and the amount of self-harm he was imposing upon himself, he did make the decision to employ a "tough-love" policy and did remove his son from his home. As was foreseen, this had a positive effect on the boy when he was faced with the responsibility of self-support. The lad began making efforts to shape up and eventually got off drugs and his relationship with his parents was greatly strengthened.

You can read consequences of parental acts through your client as well as the current condition. The more you read, the better you become, and the better you will be able to advise those in need. If someone wants to either become involved with someone else or separate from someone, you can see the fallout from either perspective.

When giving advice, you must consider that counselors must be licensed in many states, and you cannot call yourself a professional "counselor" without having a license to do so. Stick with "psychic reader" and give advice to your client only during the course of your readings. If the client needs deep and involved help, refer him to a qualified therapist for more involved work. Your readings will only involve a short amount of time, and you cannot expect someone to release emotional holds involving many years in one brief reading session. However, it can sometimes be done if the client is already on the verge of doing so and you tend to act as a catalyst.

If you detect health problems, you may ask your client to see his or her doctor as a precautionary move. Remember that you are not usually 100% accurate. Your interpretations of the imagery may be somewhat "off" due to personal feelings or previously conditioned responses to some of the images you will see. A reader certainly is not infallible and should not attempt to be more than what he or she is. Be a good or even great reader; but, as stated earlier, don't pretend to be a doctor or something that you are not trained for.

CHAPTER 9

AURAS

The human body operates at an average temperature of 98.6°F. The heat from the body can easily be seen with an infrared camera in daylight or in the dark. The metabolism of food by the body keeps the temperature constant, and the heat radiates from the inside of the body outward and dissipates with distance from the body. The human aura operates in much the same way.

The aura is like a field or glow surrounding living things. It has been photographed by Kirlean photography emanating from humans, animals, plants and other living things, The human body has an electrical system, and electric current flows through the nerve centers and neural connections throughout the entire body. This energy field can be seen by the naked eye under certain conditions when you know what to look for.

If you will notice Diagram "C" and figure number two, you will notice that the aura is close to the person's body. The farther away from the body you look, the less likely you will see the aura because it dissipates inversely with distance from the body. You will normally see it from one to four inches from the head or other areas of the body.

If you would like to practice reading auras, you may want to begin by having people stand in front of a white background in varying degrees of light until you achieve the best balance between your eyesight and the lighting of the room. The faint outline surrounding your subject will be the subject's aura, and you can see it plainly but it will be very subtle and not anything that is obvious until you have learned to recognize it.

Once you have begun to notice auras, you can then begin to discern the colors of the aura. Different levels of energy emit different frequencies, and these appear to the observer as aura coloration. I might say that there is more of an "implication" of color than the color itself. You may see an aura and notice that it seems to have a yellow cast to it or gold, green or any other color. The reason for this is that people are in varying stages of tiredness, illness, alertness, depression or any number of emotional states at the time that you may be reading their aura and the state of consciousness influences the color of the aura.

Tiredness will seem to give the aura a dark tint. You may see brown, off-white, or even black. If your subject is into healing, you may see the aura tinted a medium or light blue.

DIAGRAM "C"

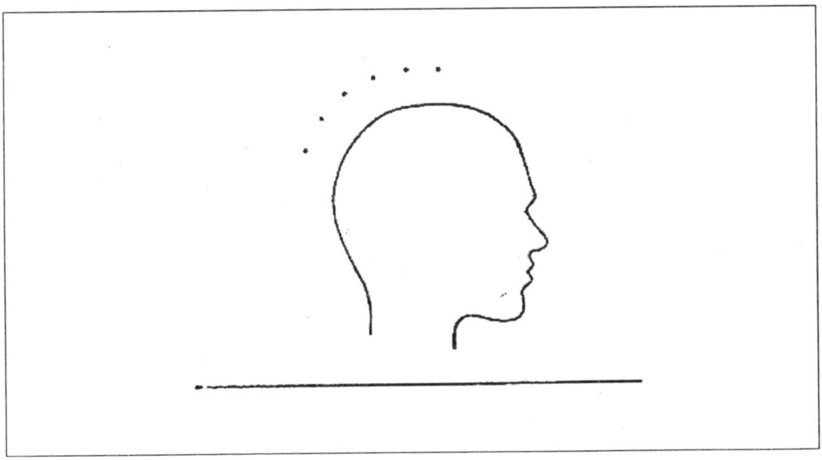

Figure 1

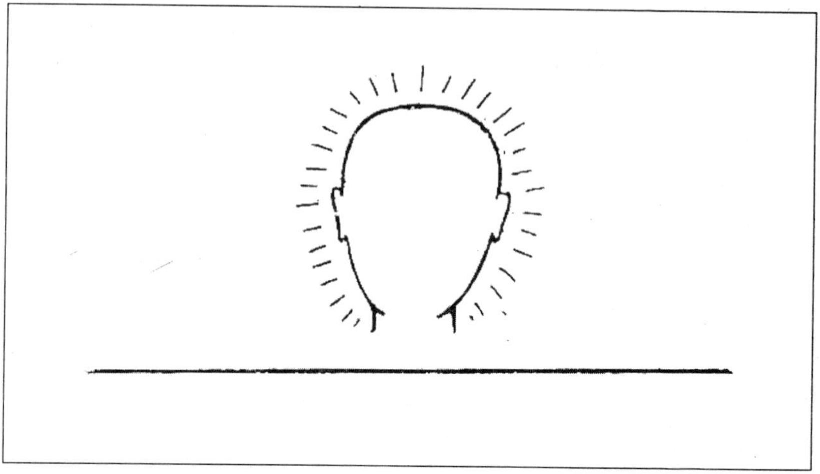

Figure 2

I was giving a lecture at a famous university and a gentleman asked me if I could see his aura, and I remarked that it looked blue. He stated that he was a dentist and thoroughly enjoyed helping people through his profession.

White auras tend to indicate people involved with spiritual matters. Spirituality is also reflected in other colors such as gold, green, white, purple and blue. Green is also associated with wealth and money interests. Black can represent extreme tiredness or severe illness and, in many cases, deceit or evil intent. Brown is earthy and illustrates interests in physical comforts and material things of life.

Not all colors represent the same thing to every person. A human being is made up of many cross conflicts and ideas. Many colors may intermix and produce off-shades, which could mean many things, or on the other hand, may be incapable of interpretation. This discussion is provided here to be used as only a guideline to get you started and allow you to explore new mysteries. Once you get into the study of auras, you will find volumes of books that have been written concerning this aspect of reading other people. It is adjunctive to psychic readings if you want to look into it.

CHAPTER 10

SELF-FULFILLING PROPHECY

One favorite technique that I frequently use during hypnotherapy is to have my clients visualize themselves in a future situation completely free of the problem they came in for. For smokers, I usually have them visualize themselves walking on a beach inhaling fresh ocean air and enjoying renewed physical energy and vitality.

I have my clients visualize this a few months ahead, and then one year ahead, and five years into the future. This will introduce into the client's subconscious mind a strong suggestion of what his or her future will look like. It also opens up the way for these things to happen.

Once we actually mentally see ourselves in a given situation and accept it as fact, we will tend to bring this about in our lives. Once the college student has decided upon a career choice, he will bring it about through positive action resulting in a degree in his chosen major field. We tend to put into motion what we can encompass in our mind as being feasible for us on a personal level.

We will accept future images and goal realizations only insofar as we can believe that they can happen to us. I can take a man or woman from a failure environment and tell him that he can achieve success, wealth and abundance. However, as soon as I become quiet, he will go back to failure and poverty. However, if through proper hypnotherapy, his self-image is transformed in his mind to being able to encompass possible improvement in his life, then miracles can begin to happen. If we can conceive that we can achieve a goal, then it can happen! It will not happen until the subconscious can accept the image as potential fact. If negativity persists due to negative experiences as a child or from other circumstances, then the image won't "take" and nothing will be accomplished. Transforming of the inner resistance will transform lives.

What has all of this to do with psychic readings? You must remember that anyone's favorite subject is himself. When you are reading someone, you are tuning into his favorite subject and with exciting accuracy! He will become so attentive and so open emotionally that what you tell him can become similar to a hypnotic suggestion. If you make a future prediction and he believes that it will happen, it will tend to happen just because you led him to believe that it will take place.

You must remember that what is planted in the subconscious can incubate and spring up at a later date. In the story of Jonah and the whale in the Old Testament of the Bible, what is illustrated is the exact point of this discussion. Jonah is our conscious mind. The idea we hold consciously is then introduced deep within our subconscious, represented by the whale. After a period of gestation time, we will see the concrete results, represented by Jonah being thrown out upon dry land.

This is the reason why I do not ever reveal any impending death if I happen to see it coming. You can easily introduce an event into the psyche of your client, and he will anxiously anticipate the event to such a degree that he can bring it about through expectation. When you give a psychic reading, be as careful as you can to be objective and hold back any personal ideas or images of what should or should not be. Your client may be very vulnerable at this particular period of his life and especially if he believes what you are telling him.

I always tell what I see and answer my client's questions as accurately as I can. However, if I detect that my client is approaching an emotional belief state or becoming over-receptive, I change the subject and come back to the future predictions at a later time when he is more in control of his own mental processes.

It is also possible to block future events from happening to your client. In my work as a therapist, I will often instruct my client to have a dream that will pinpoint his problem and the origin to the problem. This suggestion is given while he is in hypnosis. Many times he will so anticipate the dream that he literally blocks it from happening, and it doesn't happen when it is supposed to but some time later. If you foresee that your client will come into some financial bonus, he may well try to force the issue to such a degree that he virtually destroys the mechanisms, which were in effect to bring it about. We can change our destiny by changing our actions. Altering the basic factors involved can change what can be seen as going to happen.

One example is the reading given to a young lady involving the purchase of an automobile. She had been looking at a certain car that was beige in color and a certain model. It was fully intended and arranged for her to purchase the automobile. One of my students gave her an accurate reading and described the car that she was to purchase. At the last minute, her husband showed her an entirely different car, which was red and prettier than the first one; and she bought it the same day. What you read is what is in the subconscious and not in the conscious. It can be changed by outside influences that you may not be able to tune into and, consequently, will result in some possible changes in your predictions. This is also why you are not to tell someone that your predictions are absolute and will happen without fail. I always tell my clients what I have been able to see and tell them that it may change and that they, themselves, can change it if they want to.

Your predictions will range from 80-90% accurate. Most of

what you predict will come to pass and with a high degree of accuracy.

Long-term Prophecy

I generally avoid long-term prophecy, but for some psychics it is their "cup of tea". Nostradamus made many predictions 400 years ago that have come to pass with an astonishing accuracy.

You can take a look at the future of nations or the world if you wish. If you plan to try this out, you will need to visualize the nation as a single lifeline and move ahead into the future much as you would do in reading an individual. Here you may be dealing with centuries rather than days or months. You may be able to see explosive events and scenes involving other forces or lines coming into the picture. How you interpret these lines and images is up to you and your perception. Write your predictions down and see how many of them come true.

CHAPTER 11

"Guiding" Our Psychic Readings: Focusing and Interpreting (Future Relationships)

Often when we are trying to do a psychic reading on someone or even on ourselves, we find that we are not really seeing anything. Along these lines, there are some helpful hints that we can do to increase receptivity.

First, many people find that it is helpful to be in a quiet room or a quiet area, away from distractions in order to zero in on the person who is being read. Secondly, it is helpful to concentrate on the person and to look at the person, but not directly! Rather, it is best to look "through" the person as if you are looking through and past that person to the back of the person or either to the side of the person. Do not stare at the person in the face directly. I do not require that the person speak or make any sounds, other than if I am asking a question regarding what the person may want to know specifically.

As outlined earlier, you may first begin with touching the hand lightly, although this is not necessary and proceed from there with the body scan, as to health conditions and the visualization of the lifeline. Once the lifeline is visualized, one may see images in the future or in the past on the lifeline, as desired.

Once you see the lifeline, say in the future, isolate that image out and look at it more closely. For example, a student in one of our classes was doing a reading on another person and saw a woman from the back only and noted that her hair was blonde in a long wide braid. That was all that the reader could see. She was asked then to turn the woman around and see what she saw. She did this and noted that the woman was holding a bouquet in her hands. All she could see was the bouquet, and she described the flowers in great detail. Then she saw the woman's dress and saw that it was a long formal-type dress.

She was then asked to see if she could perceive where the woman was. She then saw her standing in an aisle between what appeared to be the pews of a church, near the front. She was asked to look at the rest of the room and relate what she saw. She then saw persons sitting in the pews about three or four deep down near the front of the church.

As she continued to interpret her images and read additional images, she described an old man in a white robe and recognized that he was the minister. She described him in great detail. She then looked further into the images and saw a couple kneeling on a kneeling bench and the white wedding dress of the bride and the morning coat of the groom. It was not until she got to this part of the reading that she knew for sure that it was a wedding, and then she recognized the people in the wedding.

Only by "guiding" the reading, was this reader able to let the entire scene unfold. She saw each part at the time and then was able to put it together. Sometimes this will happen in psychic readings. If you only see one thing, that does not mean that that is all there is. You should try to see more. Have your subject ask questions and see if you can see more or ask yourself questions to see if you can enhance your visual images.

Never assume that something is there if it is not. Never jump to conclusions about what is happening. Without the whole reading in this case, it would not have been possible to tell exactly what was going on whether it was a christening, a general church event or a community event utilizing the church or another event. As more and more unfolded, the event became clearer and clearer as well as the participants. Some of the participants were unknown, and some of the faces were not seen. However, several were seen and recognized. Also, never try to interpret or make a reading be what you want it to be or think that it should be.

There is one psychic who is very good at visualizations, but lacks the patience to determine what the visualizations or images mean and will try, consequently, to make an interpretation when he does not have enough information or does not know enough details. He will interpret what he thinks it means or what he thinks it should mean, and in so doing, often misinterprets.

For example, in doing a reading, if you see a little child running in front of a car in the future, do not tell the person that I see your child being injured in a car accident in the future. First, describe the child and ask the subject if he or she knows a child of that description. It may be a neighbor's child or an acquaintance's child or a relative's child. Then, based on whether you may want to actually reveal something so traumatic, go ahead and tell the subject what you have seen. You may say (if it is for example, the subject's sister's child) that there is danger in the future from a car in the street, or something similar.

If you see a wedding, for example, as the reader described earlier did, do not tell the person that he or she is getting married unless you are able to ascertain that for a fact. You may say that it is someone close to him or that you feel that it is someone close to him, but that you cannot see clearly who it is. But if you see clearly who it is, then describe the person and ask the subject if he knows who that is.

If you can only, for example, see the church and know that a ceremony is going on inside, say that; do not go ahead and say there may be a funeral or a wedding or a christening. Just tell what you see unless you do see more.

If you happen to see your subject standing with a man or woman in the future, describe the man and ask the subject if he or she knows this person. If they are standing close, then say so; do not say this is your husband or wife unless you see that, as we have seen in the case of the actual wedding revelation. The person you see may be a person who will become important in your subject's life, but without becoming the subject's spouse.

When reading relationships, the important thing is to read exactly what is seen without embellishment, without attempts at interpretation that are beyond your capability at the present time. Often, what may not be seen on a certain date may be seen at a later date. A reading may become clearer as time goes by if the person has an updated reading.

All of this depends on how much a person consults a psychic or is read or how much the person desires to be read. There are some persons who require only one reading and are completely satisfied. Others have a need for frequent readings and perhaps by various psychics.

You must also consider that what one psychic may see is at a different angle than what another psychic may see, but it may all be part of the same picture. Therefore, if two or three different psychics read you and one gives a totally different reading about your future than another has given with no similarities whatsoever, then you should perhaps consider that one of the psychics is off base. No two will see exactly the same things, but there should be some similarities in some ways.

That is how one may test a new psychic. If this one tells a person nothing that sounds plausible or nothing that has ever been stated or seen before, then perhaps you should have another reading by an independent psychic. Also, have a psychic read your past, to see if the person is tuned into you. If the psychic cannot tell you anything that sounds at all like you, then you have consulted a psychic who is not in tune with you. Your psychic should be able to tell you specific things about you, not general things that would fit almost anyone.

When you have a reading done by a new psychic, do not

tell the psychic anything or give him or her any clues unless the psychic asks you what you wish to know. Then you may say, "What about my love life"? or "What about my future financial situation"? Do not say, "I am thinking about divorcing my husband and I have another man whom I am seeing and I don't know what to do. What do you see me doing?" You have already told the psychic everything, and now all the psychic has to do is make a guess as to what you will do. In this particular case you will not be getting a true psychic reading. If you tell the psychic nothing and then ask about finances or romances, you will stand to get a truer, more objective psychic reading. You will also discover if this psychic is truly in tune with you and if you want to have a repeat visit with him at a later date.

There is another good psychic who has at times been found to misinterpret due to personal feelings of his own. For example, he was a friend with a couple that had had some marital problems, which they had kept secret. This friend, in reading the wife, saw the marital problems and the cause, but did not want to say this nor did he want to reveal what he saw for the wife in the future, as it involved a divorce and her relationship with another man. Therefore, he told her that he saw her continuing in a beautiful relationship with her husband, just as they had always had. The wife knew that this was not the case and wondered why the friend had read it this way. Later on, he confessed to her that he had seen otherwise, but didn't want to say what he really saw.

Perhaps, this makes the point that we should not read friends in a lot of cases; and as we have stated earlier, it is often the case that we are not able to read our friends or relatives as well as we may be able to read total strangers. If you are reading a friend and feel that you might be influenced to change the reading or color what you really see, then it would be better if you did not read this person and left it for him or her to consult an independent psychic.

As mentioned earlier, there was a talented psychic who was able to read and see her husband's ongoing affair. This precipitated the end of their marriage, or apparently so. Perhaps it was better that it come to a "head", so to speak, earlier rather than later. However, without having any preconceived notion or warning that this might be the case, the wife had been able through her psychic powers to determine just what was going on and why her marriage had deteriorated. In spite of the fact that she was a good psychic, she, nevertheless, was taken aback by her own readings and felt just as disturbed afterwards as any woman would have felt who had learned that her husband was currently having an affair.

There was another female psychic, who in reading a couple who were her friends, saw that they would shortly be getting a divorce. However, like the gentleman described earlier, she altered her readings and told both the husband and the wife, in independent readings, that she saw them having a marvelous marriage and staying together. Both felt that this was not possible and wondered how she could see that when they both had in mind to get a divorce at an early date and had in fact drawn up a contract. Later on, this psychic admitted that she had not wanted to tell them what she really saw because she wanted them to stay together.

Such readings are of no benefit to anyone because in such cases, the party or parties will sense that the psychic is not being straight with them. Also, this will not help the friendship. Therefore, think very carefully before you rush into reading friends or relatives and looking into their most intimate lives.

If you do read a close friend or relative and see something amiss or intimate, it is perhaps best for you to say that you cannot see anything, rather than to try to change what you do actually see and make it the way you feel would be right. We have a friend who is an excellent psychic, but when faced with situations as above, she will say, "Oh, I am just not tuning in today. Sometimes, I can tune in and sometimes, I can't." Then she will jokingly add, "I am what you call just an off and on reader." Actually, she is a very astute psychic and hardly ever misses anything.

In conclusion, we see what may be seen. Sometimes, we may

be able to see only bits and pieces. At other times, we may be able to describe people in great detail, just as if that person were actually sitting right there in front of us. On the other hand, as we have already discussed, some psychics are more tuned into feelings about how things will turn out rather than seeing what will happen.

If you practice the techniques, which have been outlined earlier, you will soon develop your own particular strengths as a psychic reader. Then you will notice that you are able to read accurately in certain areas and perhaps less accurately in others. If there is any area that you may feel that you are less competent in, then concentrate on the other areas.

For example, you may be astounding at describing future relationships right down to the tip of the nose and the color of the eyes, but you may have trouble with past readings. Or you may be excellent at doing body scans, but you may have trouble tuning into performance readings on a person's car or his stock portfolio. If you have little prior knowledge of the stock market and its functioning or of the mechanical workings of an automobile, then it might well be difficult for you to be good in readings along these lines.

If you have no interest in the body or its functions and have never really thought about it, you might have difficulty tuning into "health readings". However, you will be able to find areas wherein you may excel. You may, for example, be strong in the area of future readings and happenings. You may even be sound oriented and "hear" rather than "see" revelations. If you have art ability, you may use your psychic power to do "psychic drawings". You may team up with law enforcement to draw persons whom they are seeking. Or you may use your psychic art to draw loved ones whom your subjects are seeking or even loved ones who are now departed but were important to them in the past.

There are endless possibilities along these lines, and if your utilization of psychic talents works for you and you are able to utilize it in a way that is of benefit to others, then this is an ability and talent just like any other. Once you have the basic skills, use these to branch out and develop your own area of expertise and then you will be well on your way to becoming the best you can be.

An example of psychic art can be found in a reading wherein a young man whose young bride had died prematurely (at age eighteen) came in. The young husband was distraught and had no pictures of his bride due to an elopement and her having been orphaned at an early age. He, therefore, consulted a psychic artist in the hopes of having his late wife's likeness re-created. The psychic whom he contacted happens to be a very gifted psychic along these lines and had no difficulty in producing a remarkable portrait of the deceased young lady.

CHAPTER 12

Psychic Intervention

Can you intervene in someone's life through proper visualization techniques? Can you make changes happen in your client's life without his permission or knowledge? Can you intervene at will?

To answer the above questions, we must first consider that what you are initially doing is reading what is going to happen under normal circumstances and without deliberate intervention on anyone's part. However, it is an intriguing thought that you may alter someone's destiny through your own visualization techniques. Whether you can do this depends upon several factors.

You will remember that your client is in a receptive state of mind and fully capable of incorporating your suggestions into his psyche and bringing about the prophecy through sheer faith in what you are saying. Therefore, it is reasonable that you can give a reading as you see it, discuss the situation with your client and, with his cooperation, make changes in the imagery.

I have read people in whom I saw much confusion and continued depression. Upon discussion of the problem at hand, they agreed to visualize clarity of purpose and future improvement. When they did just that, they improved! One lady was so depressed over the death of her husband that when her problem was talked out with her and new options were discussed with her and she was asked to re-visualize her future, she did so with enthusiasm and changed her life drastically.

We all have freedom of choice and can plant new ideas and carefully selected images in our subconscious, and they will manifest in our lives as improvement and change selected by our conscious mind. Most people never avail themselves of this option and continue to muddle through life governed by subconscious images planted in their mind during childhood by those in control at that time. Unless they choose to change those images, your reading will be followed exactly as you see it and what you predict will occur.

Can you, through your imaging process, insert new imagery and cause it to become reality in someone's life without his cooperation? The answer to this question is "sometimes yes and sometimes no". It depends upon how much rapport you have with your client and to what degree of intensity and clarity you can form the image.

The technique for this is to visualize your new image near the lifeline of your client and then see it merge into one. If your client's subconscious receptivity is such that he accepts the new image at his subconscious level, then you have affected a change. If the subconscious is blocking anything external to him, then your efforts will be in vain.

Controlled meditation utilizes the basic principle just described. The technique teaches the meditator to enter his own subconscious mind and then visualize the intended beneficiary as being perfectly well and healthy. You are to continue this practice until you feel that you have no further need to meditate and then bring yourself out of the meditative state. You are not to dwell on any ill condition or negativity. Dwell only on complete correction of whatever is affecting your client or meditative recipient. The degree to which this will work depends upon the ability of the recipient to receive positive or improvement imagery. If the problem is due to a guilt complex or internal desire to die, then you will not get through and will notice no results in your meditation efforts.

When you enter the subconscious and mentally create loving images and uplifting thought patterns for someone else, you are doing nothing more than saturating your own subconscious with the same thoughts you wish for your client. In so doing, you will also benefit from your own meditation, which you have intentionally directed for the benefit of others.

When giving psychic readings, you are generally neutral and report just what you see and nothing more. However, there will be times when you will want to enter the meditative state and impart an uplifting experience for your client and can do so through the techniques you have learned. Your motives must be of sincerest honesty and openness. The result of your efforts will be immediately reflected in your life as well as in the life of your client. When you fill your mind with love, health, abundance, wealth, achievement and other positive energy changes for someone else, you can't help but be uplifted by your own thoughts. Many techniques and specific procedures for psychic intervention will be outlined in greater detail in Part II.

CHAPTER 13

SEPARATING IMAGINATION FROM PSYCHIC PERCEPTION

There is no more vulnerable an area for misinterpretation than reading a client for romantic or sexual compatibility purposes. The reason for this is that psychics, like anyone else, have their own personal problems, strong points and weak points. A psychic may be reading a client and have much the same problem that his or her client has. The psychic may become so empathetic that he or she begins to allow his or her own needs to cloud the overall picture and influence the images that are supposed to be for the client.

There is a psychic who has had so much personal loneliness that it affects her reading. She tends to give readings that are much like what she wants them to be rather than what they actually are. There was another psychic who always told his clients that someone was going to break into their house and that they should change all of the locks in the house for their own protection. He was very old, lived alone and was merely projecting his own subconscious fears into his readings. When you read someone close to you, there will be a tendency to block out certain areas and interject personal desires into your reading. This is why it is usually better for close loved ones to have a reading done by a total stranger rather than a family member.

How do you avoid this problem? How do you keep your own fantasies and personal wishes out of the picture in order to afford your client a true unbiased reading? In order for you to become a professional psychic with any degree of reputation or credibility, you absolutely must master the techniques for separation of personal fantasy from psychic perceptions.

As you begin to read lifelines and employ the techniques as described earlier, you will realize that there is little to no room for personal fantasy. When you picture the oval area on the wail or heart area, you will be utilizing a technique that will allow clear images to form within that framework. The images will tend to be images associated with the person whom you are reading. There is nothing to prevent you from interjecting your own pictures or images into the background scene, but you will have to will it to be so. You will soon learn which is which and how to keep your own impressions from interfering with the overall psychic impressions.

Psychic impressions are all around us and come from many sources including our own thoughts and desires. When you begin to read other people, you will become aware of the difference between your thoughts and those from outside sources. It will take practice and patience; but, with time, it can be accomplished.

The techniques and mental imagery props that I have described will work for you. Use the same prop every time and as you notice new and different images with each person you read, you will soon come to appreciate the true value of the techniques you have been taught. It can be compared to the format used in writing a book. The paper in each book is almost identical; the sizes of books vary but are all within easy handling size. However, the content of each book is different. Once you have become familiar with the vehicle, the content will change with each individual reading you do.

There will be techniques that you will initially use, but some of them will change as you progressively move forward in your reading skills; and you will eventually develop your own techniques which will work for you better than any other method. As long as it works for you and you are able to give highly accurate readings, then more power to you. However, there will be times when you may wander so far from the main path that your readings become confused and difficult. If that time ever comes, it is time to go back to basics for a while until you are once again on track.

You may encounter times when you cannot read at all. You may see little to nothing or may see only your own imagination's imagery. At this time it may be well for you to back away and take a break for a while. Pushing yourself into reading when you don't feel like it or are not able to tune in properly will result in an inadequate reading at best. If this happens, it is far better to take a mental respite for a few days, weeks, or months until you are again emotionally prepared to handle your readings with freshness and clarity.

CHAPTER 14

INTUITIVENESS

Intuitiveness deals with having the ability to sense, hear or perceive things rather than being able to see images or interpret impressions. There will be many times when you may or may not see an image but will have to go on your "gut feelings". You will see something in the lifeline of your client and absolutely be unable to interpret the meaning of what you see. In cases like this you will be able to pick up a "feeling" or "awareness" of the answer. Many times I will be asked a question, and I will sense or feel the answer rather than see anything. This is why it is better to read perfect strangers rather than someone you are emotionally close to. It is easier to separate your own feelings when reading a stranger than when reading your wife or husband or other close friend or relative.

There is no mental framing to use as a prop when you are being intuitive. However, adopting the proper mental posturing is helpful because your attitude is one of attunement with your client's need at the time.

I remember reading in a fair when a lady walked up, and I immediately began to think of travel. As she sat down, I told her that "travel" surrounded her and she related that she was interested in going into travel as a profession. I did not see any images or any types of normal mental props nor did I use any techniques described in this book. The word "travel" came into my mind with no association of visual imagery whatsoever.

I was reading a lady at another fair when the name "John" popped into my mind. I asked her who "John" was, and she remarked that he was her ex-husband with whom she had been having problems. The name came into my mind totally unexpectedly and without effort. The first time this happened to me was long before I became aware that I would develop my reading talent into a profession.

A friend and I were attending an antique auto auction, and I was standing next to a nicely dressed young lady. During the auction I suddenly became aware of a name but didn't say anything to her. Shortly a friend of hers came up and called her by her name, and it was the same name that I had mentally heard several minutes before. How many times have you been engaged in conversation with someone only to know in advance what he or she was about to say? How many times have you known ahead of time what was about to happen in any given situation? How many times have you sensed what was going on without any other clues whatsoever?

Some people are not visionary people but still can become excellent psychic readers. They have to develop their intuitive receptiveness to a higher degree and learn to depend on it to a greater extent than someone who can "see" visual imagery. Some of the people you will read will be of this type. They will be total "feelers" and will go on feelings alone and have little to no mental ability to visualize anything. Strange as it may seem, I know an artist of some years' experience who paints professionally but cannot visualize any picture before she paints it. However, she goes on feelings and produces beautiful landscapes, still life, abstracts and impressionistic paintings. If you are not a visual person, you can develop sensitivities in other areas of receptivity.

As you have undoubtedly discovered by now, the term "psychic power" is a total misnomer. There is not "power" involved in psychic readings at all. Being able to read someone psychically is to be able to become extremely receptive to subtle impressions of which we are surrounded daily. I am reminded of advertisements that tout certain radios as being "powerful" when what is meant is that they can pick up broadcasts farther away than other radios. They are not "powerful" but are significantly more "sensitive" to weak signals than other radios. The same holds true about psychics.

There will be times when you see visual images and will totally misread what you see. The images and pictures are there, and if you go totally on imagery, you will misread some of them. When you get to an image you are having difficulty interpreting, stop for awhile and become aware of your intuitive awareness and try to sense what this image means to your client. Remember that you are reading your client, not your own personal interpretation of what the images mean for you.

CHAPTER 15

Case Histories

In my many years of professional experience with countless persons, many interesting case histories have manifested themselves as being worthy of inclusion in this volume.

We have seen that psychic readings may be used as a prognosticator of illness or healthiness in a potential mate or lover. Along this line, a young lady came into the office for a reading. She had been having some general health problems, nothing specific, and was not getting any better. In the course of the reading, it was noted that she had a large red area in her chest, specifically on the left breast. She was advised to see her gynecologist for a complete work-up. In so doing, it was not pointed out to her that she might possibly have a problem in the left breast in order not to alarm her; but rather, she was merely told that it would be advisable for her to have a complete check by her gynecologist. Later, she called back to say that mammograms had revealed some tumors in her left breast, which upon examination, were found to be benign, but felt to be potentially dangerous by her doctor. These were excised and now she is on periodic follow-up by her doctor, but is doing well and is reassured.

A friend of a student from one of our classes had another

friend of many years who had apparently suddenly become ill and was hospitalized. All of his family stated that he had pneumonia. The student who had developed into quite a good psychic was asked to give a reading concerning the possible improvement of health of the hospitalized man. All that he saw during the reading was a solid red background all the way around the lifeline and the specter of the Death Angel hovering overhead. The psychic knew then that the man was terminally ill. Through creative visualization, he psychically removed the Death Angel and visualized a healthy white lifeline for the ill man. It was effective in that for a few days, the family stated that the man was improving. However, he relapsed after that and did indeed die. It was later confirmed that he had died of AIDS.

In another vein, psychic readings may be seen to forecast future events involving relationships. A supposedly happily married young lady came in for a reading and the imagery revealed a fantasy-type encounter with a handsome young man, involving a great deal of chemistry between the two and very romantic and sexual lovemaking. When the young man was described, she confirmed that she did know such a man and was highly desirous of an involvement with him and that she, in fact, had had an affair with him in the past. The future imagery revealed that she and he would be together again in the future; and she left happy, but with a decision to make regarding her present marriage.

Even though this reading was quite explicit, nothing specifically salacious was revealed to the young lady, but the point was made and she understood the meaning of the imagery without great details being provided.

One married lady who is an excellent psychic and is also a former student from our classes was unhappy in her third marriage, but did not know the problem until one day she visualized her husband with another woman. She then knew that her husband was having an affair and confronted him with it, describing the woman in great detail in the process. This struck a nerve with her husband; but he refused to admit to her that she was right, calling her a "witch" and other names in the process. She was proven right, however, when shortly thereafter this woman was indeed revealed to be his lover, and he asked for a divorce.

There are those who say, "Do we want this ability to see other relationships such as affairs our spouses or lovers are involved in?" "Do we want to see what is in the future when it may not be the way we want it to be?" I always answer such persons by saying that what we are to see, I believe, is revealed to us only if we are supposed to see these things. Some things we may see; others we may not be able to see. We all have the potential to change our future, if so desired, even after a reading. In some cases, a reading concerning future relationships might be of benefit and comfort to someone who is lonely and truly desirous of a good relationship.

There are those who say, "I would not want to be able to have my spouse read me. Maybe there are some things that I do not want my spouse to know." I answer these persons by saying that in most cases, we are unable to read persons that we are extremely close to as well as we can read strangers. We may be able to "see" some things, but often due to a lack of objectivity, we are not able to see all things. We certainly are never able to read another person's thoughts per se. Also, it is more difficult to interpret a reading one might give someone close to him even if the imagery appears.

However, this is not to say that it cannot be done. I know of a case wherein a husband and wife who are both psychics have been able to read many things in their lives, both concerning them together and also separately. This, in many cases, has proven to be of benefit to them for the future. The mutual experiences have benefited their relationship considerably.

In another case, a professional woman came in for a reading. She was seen to have no one in her heart when the visual imagery concerning the picture on the wall was done. There was a man in the picture frame with her but he was in the background off to the side and appeared to be in a different plane from her. This was explained to her, and the man was described. She acknowledged that this was her husband and that they were truly in "different planes" and that their relationship was not getting any better. She was contemplating divorce, but had hesitated due to their respective positions.

On another occasion, a young man was being read. There were two women who were visualized on his lifeline. The first one was described to him, and he acknowledged that this was his girlfriend. The second girl whom he appeared to have a stronger feeling for was also described, but she was identical in appearance to the first girl except that she had dark short straight hair whereas the first girl had curly short blonde hair. It was as if the first girl were the second girl in a wig. The young man stated that this was his girlfriend's twin sister and that this was precisely how she looked. He also stated that he was much more attracted to the sister than to his girlfriend, but was unable to establish a relationship with the sister. However, this was keeping him from commitment to the other young lady.

Sometimes, a psychic feeling of potential negativity or danger may serve to protect us. A psychic friend had moved to a remote area in the mountains. As was her custom, she liked to go for long walks in the woods, often five or more miles, climbing uphill and fording creeks and even crossing rivers.

A few months after she had moved to the mountains and on one of her long hikes, she noted that a house that was in the process of being completed was now occupied. Her walk brought her close to the house. She proceeded on her way and completed her long hike but on the way back, she again had to pass close to this house. Her companion stated that he would like to go in and greet the new owner of the house, but my friend had a very eerie feeling regarding this and begged him to walk on past and not approach the house.

Just as they were almost beyond the house, someone came up behind them and in so doing startled them. He stated that he was the owner of the house and wanted to know what they were doing there and how they had crossed the river. My friend immediately saw an image of the devil above the man's right shoulder. She also saw images involving drug use and intimate involvement with other men surrounding this individual.

She felt such a strong satanic presence that after her and her companion's brief exchange with the owner, she vowed never to go past the house again. However, not long after that, they were curious and walked within sight of the house. Upon so doing, they observed that there were several young men around, and they were using drugs and caressing one another. Also, not far from the house, large traps and boxes had been set for catching animals and a clearing had been dug out in a circle. This, to my friend, confirmed the earlier images that she had seen. She has not returned to the area since that time. She states that she is only too glad that she had the psychic revelations because without them, she might have placed herself in danger.

Another friend visited a distant city and stayed in a "bed and breakfast" run by a middle-aged lady who professed psychic powers. This friend, being psychic herself, was enchanted by the idea of staying in the house of another psychic and maybe exchanging notes.

During the night my friend sensed a very evil presence in the house. She felt that there had been a murder or unnatural death in the very room that she was in and that one of the portraits on the wall was involved. She was unable to look at this picture of a woman in the portrait without seeing death portrayed in the image.

Also, the "psychic" owner of the house was speaking of "little men dressed in black" who came down from the ceiling and whose feet stuck out of the ceiling. These men supposedly told her what to do and often took over for her when she was speaking and "helped" her out. She had, it turned out, seances in the room adjoining but open to the room my friend had stayed in.

Was there either evil in the house or a dark force in the room? There were two other persons who accompanied my friend on the trip who also felt the presence of evil. The feeling was so strong that they were unable to spend another night in the house.

An acquaintance came in for a reading. After her reading was completed, she recounted a health experience that she had had in years past. She had been lying in bed and had an image appear in her mind in which her departed grandmother had said to her, "If there is a rotten apple in the barrel, take it out, or all of the apples will soon be rotten."

The lady pondered the vision and took it to mean that she had better go have her health checked. After a physical, it was found that she had had a "questionable" Pap test. The doctor stated, "It is probably all right." However, the lady kept hearing the words of her grandmother, and she knew that she needed to have a hysterectomy.

She went back and told the doctor, and he said, "All right, if that is what you feel." As it turned out, she had cancer of the uterus; and by following the psychic vision she had had of her grandmother, she had perhaps saved her own life.

Another case involved a young man who had strong psychic visions of his grandmother and felt that she was always with him. On one occasion, he saw her on one side of him and a young lady on the other side. He had not seen the young lady in several years, but after the psychic vision, he felt that his grandmother was telling him to contact the young lady. He did so and found that this young lady had wanted to contact him but did not know how. They started dating and were soon engaged to be married.

There was another case in which a young professional male came in for a reading. In the course of the reading, he was seen to have many female images in his "heart picture". There was a picture of one primary female, but images of many others kept coming and going. This was revealed to him, and he finally admitted that he had had a succession of affairs even though he was married and loved his wife and that he was presently involved in an affair. His future looked much the same as his past – a continuous succession of affairs. As far as I know, to this day, this man is still not faithful to his wife.

There was a lady who requested a reading for romantic purposes. She wanted to know about any future involvement, as she and her husband had just recently been divorced. The images that were seen indicated that she would be remarried in a Southern church with a steeple wherein the bells were visible from the street. The inside of the church was described in detail as was the general make-up of the guests on each side of the aisle.

The preacher was described as being older with thin hair and balding on the top of his head. Her ex-husband and her children were at the ceremony as well as her future husband's friends and relatives. After the ceremony they all went into the reception area, and it was described right down to the dark paneling on the walls.

This scene was read, not only by myself, but by two other psychics as well and each described the scene in almost identical details. One saw the church and described it with the ceremony, the other saw the reception area and the third psychic saw the entire scene. As of this printing, the lady is still awaiting the outcome of the readings.

In another case, a young lady was read who was having a great deal of frustration and difficulty in a current relationship. She was desperate to find any hope in the future for her and the man. In the reading, the man in whom she was interested was seen as having a yellow lifeline, turning brown and murky at times. She went on to relate that he had acted in a peculiar manner and had strange mood changes. One minute he would be very nice, and the next he was saying irrational things and would become very agitated with apparently no reason. After attempting to continue the relationship for a while longer, she discovered that he was mentally unbalanced and suffering from a nervous disorder. The lifeline reading was accurate.

Another lady obtained a reading for her career objectives. She related that she was taking a real estate course and planned to enter into real estate on a full time basis. The reading indicated that she would not be selling real estate but would venture into another job doing essentially the same type of work but with another company. This is what happened within two months from the time of the reading.

During a student practice session, I had each student give readings beginning with one side of the room and allowing students to read each other. During the course of the readings one gentleman, whom I shall call Sam, gave a man, whom I shall call John, a reading. Sam told John that he saw a woman nearby. However, he stated that he also saw another person like a shadow behind the first woman; and he felt that it, too, was a woman.

John began to squirm in the chair and blush and desired to change the subject. He didn't comment on the reading, and the readings continued around the room. Later John told me that Sam had picked up on the girl behind the scenes and that no one had previously suspected the clandestine affair he had been having for some time now. He said that Sam, whom John had never met before nor had any reason to have any contact with previously, was 100% accurate in his perception.

Bill, a student who liked to work on cars and was familiar with the inner workings of automobiles, was asked to see if he could pick up anything on a certain automobile which he never had seen or been given any information on. Bill visualized the car and described discoloration in the transmission area of the vehicle. The car in question had, in fact, been giving trouble in the transaxle (transmission) for only a few days, and no one in the class had any knowledge concerning the problem.

When it was Jane's turn to read, she described another student's girl friend. In the process, she described another girl that Bill, the student, said was his girlfriend's sister. Jane saw both women clearly and accurately determined which one was Bill's girlfriend.

During a psychic fair, I had been giving a number of readings when a lady came over to the table for a reading. I immediately heard music and singing, and I related this to the lady. She told me that she was a singer and was considering going into singing for a profession and was going to ask me questions concerning this matter. My impression was that she should continue to pursue her singing career but to do so part-time for a while longer and then go into full time singing. She did and was very successful.

Another lady I read at the fair asked about her father. She gave me neither details nor any further information. I saw a lifeline close to her decline and terminate, and I told her what I saw. I also told her that the lifeline looked yellow (indicating medication) and that it was growing very faint and did not seem to come back up but did terminate. She then related to me that her father was suffering from cancer and was not expected to live. I also perceived that her lifeline was very shallow and had a yellow tint due to emotional strain and worry. She confirmed the accuracy of the reading.

While reading at a Shriner's Bazaar years ago, a lady came for a reading who was a skeptic but still curious. She was wearing many large diamonds and beautiful jewelry and was seemingly in a jovial spirit. However, upon beginning the reading I perceived that she was unhappy and seeking purpose in her life. I then saw an off-white wedding dress and stated that I saw marriage plans and anticipation of a wedding soon. She then related that she was very unhappy but she was dating a gentleman and was planning a wedding, and I had described the exact gown she had planned to use in the wedding.

Another lady asked questions concerning her husband's business. When doing the reading, I suddenly saw another lifeline near hers that was yellow; and I began to describe this line. I felt that she was much more concerned about this person with the yellow line than she was about her husband's business. I saw the yellow gradually clear and brighten up and return to normal. She then related that she had just brought her mother home from the hospital and that she was sick but in the process of recovery. She stated that she had been very worried about her mother and was glad to hear that she would be all right.

Another lady just asked me to tell her whatever I could see. I told her about her past boyfriend and how the relationship had gone. I told her that I saw another man in the future, and

I saw a wedding for them. I felt that they were already dating. She said that the reading was totally accurate. She and her new boyfriend were planning to marry in two months.

In another reading, a gentleman placed his hands in mine, and I immediately felt that one hand was warmer than the other was. I pictured his body image and noted that much blackness was located in the heart area and upper chest. When I described what I had seen mentally, he stated that he had suffered from a heart attack some time back and was experiencing circulatory problems now. Looking forward along the lifeline, I saw much improvement in the future for him.

A man requested a second reading a few months after the first. He stated that he had not believed what I hat said was going to happen; but when he met a small child who changed his life in many ways, he remembered that I had predicted this some months back. He returned wanting to hear more.

One lady was in for a reading, and I saw total emptiness in her heart but with many faces and/or images around the heart area. I interpreted this to mean that she had many friends and loved ones but no one who filled her needs on a close personal level. She stated that, indeed, she had many friends and relatives who were very close. However, she was divorced and had no husband nor was she dating anyone and was very lonely. She asked concerning romance in her future, and I told her my impressions of future events. She later related that many predictions had come to pass.

During a recent reading, I perceived many disturbances in the lifeline of my client that occurred when she was about ten years old. I saw much emotional variation and upheaval with this event clouding her present mental state. Upon further discussion, she remembered being molested at that age and having suffered emotional turmoil. She followed up with this and underwent therapy. Once the guilt was removed and she dealt with the problem, her attitude improved drastically and she overcame her problem quite successfully.

One of the most interesting readings I have ever participated in was between Jane and Mary, two students that met each other the first time in one of my classes.

Jane had been regressed through hypnosis into a previous life experience wherein she described a beautiful antebellum home, beautiful furnishings, grounds, etc. She lived in the house during the Civil War but was murdered by two renegade Union soldiers who broke into the house, caught her hiding behind the door, and cut her throat. Her remembrances were vivid and real to her but once the emotions had subsided she was able to describe an area north of Natchez, Mississippi, and named her parents, relatives and the young man to whom she was betrothed. I mention the hypnotic regression for a reason.

Mary began to read Jane one night on the phone while they were discussing the class, but what was strange was that she began reading about a life during the Civil War era. Mary described the exact scene that Jane had described but with additional details and with details from a different physical angle. Everything was exact. The colors, the description of the murdered body being found, the burial, the description of the betrothed and his reaction to the murder were identical. This entire reading was done without having any prior knowledge of the regression that Jane had recently undergone. What had started as a casual reading between two friends startled both of them because they discovered that they had lived concurrently in the nineteenth century and on the same Southern plantation.

So many details were described during the reading and the regression that Jane and Mary actually went to an area north of Natchez and discovered many names and facts, which verified both the regression and the reading.

In another case, a friend of mine asked me to read someone through him. I saw his friend's lifeline ascend in a healthy and normal manner with clarity and normal brightness. Then, however, the line flared and stopped abruptly. He said that his friend had been accidentally electrocuted while working on a piece of equipment.

On a recent trip out of town, I asked my wife to visualize the van my son and I were to travel in and see if she could perceive any potential problems. She said that one of the rear tires seemed to have a problem. At the time the tires looked fine so we drove out of town. On the way my son, who was only nine at the time, practiced the imagery and told me that we would have trouble with a rear tire. Sure enough, a nail was found embedded in the left rear that caused a loss of air.

On another occasion my wife said that something "in the middle of the engine" looked as though it might be causing trouble. Within a few days, the heater by-pass hose blew out and stranded me miles from home.

While traveling on the road some years back, I hit a light tan van in the rear. It caused a good deal of damage to my car but no injuries. When I returned home, my wife told me about a vision she had experienced wherein she viewed the exact accident in detail prior to its happening. She had not told me about this when we talked on the phone because she feared that somehow telling me about an accident that was going to happen might actually cause it to happen. Also, at that time she wasn't as confident in her visions and imagery as she is now so she kept quiet about it. However, it did happen just as she had foreseen that it would.

On another occasion when my wife and I were in the mountains, she felt that she felt an immediate need to return home. She couldn't explain why she felt that way, but we returned anyway. When we got home, we discovered that a water pipe had burst; and the entire basement was flooded and water was running out the garage door.

Had she not listened to her intuitive impulses, we would have had an even greater disaster than what was evident.

Another young man was visiting a friend when he met a lady of some interest to him. He visualized the body image and focused on the pelvic area and saw a clear white translucence, which indicated health and freedom from infection or disease. He pursued the relationship.

During another class a student, whom I shall call Jim, received a reading indicating that his new business venture was going to be very successful and that the business lifeline was going up gradually over a period of time. Jim was struggling and became very discouraged many times. However, the business gradually increased and within a few months, the readings proved very accurate.

Jim was very skeptical about psychic readings and took the course only because we were friends and he was curious. However, after taking the course and observing the extreme accuracy of the students and his own readings, he became convinced and has done readings on his own since then. There were many times when he was certain that he would have to close up his new business because of lack of revenue. Now, however, he is earning more income than he has ever earned and is quite optimistic concerning his future.

A chiropractor took one of the courses and began practicing the techniques at his office. He states that he can now see conditions in his patients that the patients didn't know were there. The doctor says that he visualizes the body image and makes the diagnosis. He then uses medical equipment to see if what he sees can actually be determined and proven. If he can verify that the condition exists, he then treats his patient for that condition. He states that his rate of patient improvement has gone markedly upward, and he is a much better doctor because of his newfound techniques.

A detective took a course and related that his "hunches" are 200% more accurate than ever before. He relates how he allows images to pass before his mind concerning the case he is working on and is amazed to discover that he can often "see" the solution to his case or even a picture of the person who has committed the crime. His strengthened intuition has guided him to greater success and much increased confidence in himself.

Another student gave a reading to his girlfriend and saw redness in the chest area. His girlfriend had not experienced any chest problems previous to the reading but had to go to the doctor a few days later and was then diagnosed as having bronchitis. He made several other predictions, which did also come to pass.

A politician came to me and stated that a man in a powerful position had approached him. The man had wanted to enter a "deal" between himself and the politician, and the politician wanted to know what I saw about this possible involvement. I immediately saw a man talking with my client. However, around the image of this man I saw darkness. I felt that the darkness revealed sinister intentions and related this to my client. He later related that if he had gone ahead with the proposed plans with this man, he would have been in much trouble now because illegal dealings had been recently disclosed concerning the man in question.

On a recent TV show, I was asked about a man's current business relative to any foreseen success. I then saw two sub-lines and stated that he had two interests rather than one and that the second would soon take precedence over the first. He then stated that he had started another business that was beginning to grow faster than the one he was originally in. He felt that my reading was totally accurate.

Some readings are not so accurate. Several years ago, I was listening to an excellent psychic on a local talk show. She was amazingly accurate with names, dates etc., of the people calling in. However, a listener asked questions relative to the United States entering a war with Iraq, and she said that there would be no war. She stated that she saw "something" which would prevent any war from happening. Whether she properly interpreted the images or whether the images were not available, I can't say except to state that the normal percentage of success with psychic readings will vary from eighty percent to ninety-five percent with occasional "homeruns" of one hundred percent accuracy! I don't know of any psychic who is accurate all of the time.

I do not give national or world readings as a rule. However, when asked concerning the war, I was also curious and did attempt to foresee what would happen. I had a feeling that there would be war, but that it would not be very long-lasting. It doesn't hurt to try different things from time to time and test your accuracy. You may be surprised at your results.

One of my students gave her daughter a reading. She described a girl in her daughter's sorority as being dressed in a blue jumper with black shoes. She said that the girl had blond hair and a round face. Her daughter didn't recognize the description at first; but when she returned to college, she then remembered the girl and said that the girl was dressed exactly like the description in the reading.

There will be many times when you read that your client will not be able to place the person(s) whom you are describing but will contact you later and inform you that you were correct in your description. The image may be from the distant past when this individual had an impact on your client but has been forgotten along the way, or he may be someone in close proximity to your client such as a person at work or in a group they belong to.

Remember to tell what you see and only what you see. Do not embellish or try to make your images fit any preconceived idea that you may have of how they should or should not come out. It is not for you to be judge or jury. Be totally objective.

PART II

PSYCHIC SEX

Introduction

Over the many years of working with all types of people in all walks of life, the predominant concern of the vast majority has been in the area of romantic interests. Finances, of course, come into importance, but it is secondary when compared to the concern of people when it comes to interpersonal relationships.

Using the techniques described in Part I, "Techniques for Psychic Reading", the reader is now able to move forward and use exact techniques in specific ways. This part will illustrate in detail just how psychic power may be utilized for greater personal relationships and sexual harmony.

Since so many divorces and relationship problems are due to sexual incompatibility, blockages, abnormalities, etc., it is imperative that some method be made available to discern these types or problems beforehand. If people could somehow "sense" or "know" in advance of possible relationship problems, much heartache and discord could be avoided.

Many people are reluctant to reveal that they have diseases such as herpes, syphilis, gonorrhea, AIDS and other diseases to prospective suitors. However, if the prospective suitor can utilize the techniques contained in this book, he or she will be able to be warned in advance and make other plans accordingly.

CHAPTER 1

DETERMINATION OF SEXUAL COMPATIBILITY

In order to determine if you are compatible with someone sexually, several things are required. The first thing you must deal with is your current existing relationship with the person you want to make a determination about. If you are already close and involved, it is better that you employ someone else to do the psychic perceptions that are involved. If, however, you are not yet involved emotionally and can be an observer without prejudice mentally or emotionally, you may well be able to perform the necessary procedures to arrive at the correct answers.

Begin your investigation by tuning in to your prospective partner. Perform the lifeline reading long enough to get as clear a picture as possible. Once you have the line in your imagery, shift your attention to parallel lines and note if one of the lines consistently stays alongside this line. If this is the case, then the probability is that the relationship will be long term and consistent. Once the consistency is determined, you must actually see the physical union.

When viewing the physical union, personal desire or preference must not color your reading or you will be picking up on wishful thinking or day dreaming and not receiving the true impressions. If you are the least bit emotional about this individual, then go to another psychic and ask for his opinion concerning your intimate satisfaction with your intended partner or mate.

Let us assume that you are personally able to carry out your reading and obtain true impressions. This being the case, you can see the lifeline next to your subject and view the personal intimate exchanges as well. This image may come in the form of explicit images or may be shown symbolically. Instead of viewing intimacy, you may see hearts or varying sizes exhibiting either bright color and radiating love or pale shades and very little activity. Your interpretation of the images is crucial to the truth of what you see. Normally the highly colored hearts radiating love indicate much harmony and intimacy. The dull shades with little activity will indicate that once the honeymoon is over, very little excitement will remain.

Intimacy is a very delicate thing. It can be destroyed in the best intended of people and totally unintentionally. When you see a strong vibrant relationship extending well into the future, this is good. However, you have to look at you own lifeline as well and see if you actually have the potential to match what you see for your possible partner. If you do not have the capacity that you have seen for him or her, then letting him or her become involved with you would be just as much a mistake as the other way around.

If you see your heart in a certain light and observe your potential partner's heart and it is similar, then you may well have a compatible long-term relationship. This is why you must be uninvolved at least in the beginning.

Another way to determine sexual compatibility is to read your partner's past lifeline. As you well know, past trauma, previous emotional problems, psychological arrest factors, etc., all combine to inhibit sexual functioning and capability. If you see much turmoil in the past for your subject, you may well want to take a much closer look at his present and future lifeline.

If you are a man interested in a woman and discern that she

has been raped and traumatized in the past, you may experience mutual difficulties if you consummate the relationship. The emotional trauma may be one that she cannot deal with, and she may well experience sexual blockages due to that experience. The initial love and excitement may overcome the problem but only on a temporary basis. It will creep back in once the fire has cooled.

It is important that you scan the entire lifeline in order to make this determination. Remember that you may also have blockages in your past that will be aggravated by her problems, and your blockages may well aggravate her as well. Study the lifelines carefully, and you can sense if there is potential conflict or anticipation of harmony. If you read a man's lifeline and see a dominant maternal influence, you may rest assured that he will make his wife his mother; and when that happens, intimacy is out the window. If you observe a woman who is unusually attached to her father, she may well marry a father substitute and her intimate interest will soon suffer accordingly. Much can be learned through reading the past lifeline.

Another factor which affects marriage intimacy is how much your partner talks. If you are a quiet person and your potential partner is very talkative, you may run into conflicts. Since you like very little talk and he likes to talk all the time, you will be driven up the wall. He will also tend to talk at inappropriate times, in your judgment. In order to make this determination, visualize your potential partner in a group of people and observe his behavior. Notice if he is very talkative and notice if he likes to be the center of attention. If you notice either of these two traits in your image, you have a possible egotist who must he granted the center stage and be constantly fed for the sake of his fragile ego. If this is the case, he is to be avoided because when the going gets tough, he will lose interest in the relationship and blame you for his bruised ego.

After reading Part I, you have learned to determine your emotionality. You now should know if you are a heart-led person or head-led or anywhere in between. When you hold your potential partner's hand, you will be able to determine his or her emotionality as well. If you become involved with a heart-led person and you are head-led, you will find yourself becoming embarrassed or otherwise upset by his constant emotionalism. He will not think his way through anything but will be totally led by emotion. Incompatibility is immediately apparent in this situation.

If you are an emotional person and become involved with a restrained individual who constantly attempts to maintain control over his or her situation and you as well, this will render you upset and incompatible. Match your feeling with that of your potential mate and you will have less conflict in the future.

There was a young student who asked me to read him in reference to his relationship with his girlfriend. I saw a girl with long, dark brown hair. I saw her looking away from him in another direction and told him what I had seen. He informed me that they had just broken up, and he asked me if I thought that they would get back together. My impression was that they would not be reconciled. He later found a new partner and married her.

A lady from North Carolina came to me for a reading wanting to know about her romance possibilities with her current interest. I saw her breaking up with her current boyfriend, and I saw that another man would come into the picture within three months and she would become totally involved with him. I described the man's hair color, dress type and general features. Within a few weeks, she broke up with the man she had questioned me about. She then became involved with a man from England about three months later.

When determining compatibility, it can be either very involved or rather simple. The degree of sensitivity that you develop will be personal to you, and your ability to sense success or failure may come to you in an instant. Sometimes I know immediately even before the question is asked. At other times, I must search and balance my information before I arrive at an answer.

While I was on a TV show recently, a young lady asked me about her boyfriend. I saw his lifeline coming close to hers in the past, drifting away and becoming close once again. I related this to her, and she stated that they had been dating and had separated at one time and had just gotten back together. She asked about marriage. I saw their 1ifelines converging and going forward together. This was done within three minutes. At other times, more time for evaluation may be required.

When I had my first opportunity to enter the field of hypnotherapy as a profession, I was perplexed. I had a job with a good company and a good future, and yet I sincerely desired to become a therapist. I was listening to a psychic on radio in Atlanta and just happened to know where the location of the radio station was. I hurried to the station and met him just as he was leaving the building. I asked him if I could ask him one question, and he paused and said that he was in a hurry but he would take the question. I asked him if I should become involved in professional hypnotherapy, and his answer was "yes, it will be good for you".

One moment of time can determine entire future jobs, relationships, careers, marriages, successes or failures. Give your client your true and honest feeling. Many times it will fly in the face of reason or will go opposite of what you truly will want for yourself or your client, but you must be truthful and express exactly what you see or feel. In time, you will see the wisdom of what I have just said to you.

If you choose to see the act of sex it, continue to see it as far into the future as you can. See if the act is as exciting as you feel it should be. See if your partner is exhibiting as much true enthusiasm as is needed to maintain the relationship and observe you own responses as well.

There will be times that you will see the sex act but will notice that the entire image or a significant portion of it has darkened or even blackened out. If this is the case, then your relationship is dead or will be dead within a certain time period.

Another student was having difficulty with his girlfriend. He told me that he had lost sexual interest in her but truly wanted to regain the relationship in full. I did a reading and saw an image of the girl, but below her waist was dark. I interpreted this to mean that his interest in her sexuality was dead and could not be resurrected. This proved to be the case, and he later broke up and married another lady.

Margaret, a former student, was visiting a friend of hers at her friend's daughter's home. While there, Margaret noted the daughter's husband's lifeline and later related to her friend what she had seen. She related that his lifeline was very jagged with many ups and downs. She also sensed hostility along the line. Margaret's friend then told her that her daughter's husband was very unstable and subject to much anger and hostility. She further stated that he treated his family rather badly. Margaret also sensed that the lady would be pregnant again soon and have a baby girl. Within three months, Margaret's friend informed her that her daughter, Connie, was pregnant; and she did later have a little girl.

As you can see from the above example, someone's lifeline can be read clearly. If the lady in question had been able to psychically perceive things, she might have avoided much misery in her marriage. She might could have avoided this man in favor of a more mature man with a kind nature toward her and the family. I say "might" because people will ignore many negative things when they become involved in a romantic relationship and will often ignore red flags until it is too late.

CHAPTER 2

How to Improve Your Physical Sex Life

If you are already married or have an on-going relationship that needs a boost in intimacy, then the techniques are a little different. Your relationship may have gotten somewhat stale or you and your partner may be allowing outside influences of work, worry, other people, etc., to interfere with your personal intimate contact. People who are together much of the time will fall into this trap, and their relationship suffers from it.

One of the best ways to ease yourself into a mental posture wherein you can affect your own lifeline and that of your mate is to do so when you are reading someone else. As you are reading a client or friend, gradually visualize your own lifeline as you are reading his. I usually begin to see my own line at the end of a reading when I will have time to spend in a meditative state for my own benefit. After a reading, you are already in a receptive mood, and to continue on for your own personal reading is much easier than starting cold. Also, you are able to become detached from yourself somewhat by having read someone else.

Once you have your lifeline in mind, you can see upcoming events that can cause you emotional upset, optimism or depression. Observe the flares in the line and the general elevation and see if your line is inclining up or down. Read your line as unemotionally as possible in order to obtain an accurate future indication of what is coming toward you.

Years ago I was reading my own line when I saw light clouds surrounding my lifeline. I realized that these clouds represented money, and the clouds nearest my line represented my commissions from a job in sales. The commissions came just as I had foreseen. That is when I realized that I could read my own lifeline as well as that of anyone else.

When you have your line in mind, gradually allow the lifeline of your mate or partner to enter the picture. You will then be able to notice variances between your line and that of your mate. You can see emotional highs and lows on both lines and just where the lines are congruous and where they are not. You can also see the touching of the lines and sharing of love and emotion along the way as well as friction or irritation between the lines.

Being able to see your lifeline and that of your mate is to be able to interject change into the line and, subsequently, your future. As you gaze at the line, consciously allow positive changes to make alterations in the line. If your line sags, allow it to float upward slightly. If it is shallow and indications are that it needs to be brightened up, then allow it to be so.

Do not make drastic changes in your line, as these will not register. You can begin by making small changes; and when these have actually happened, you can move on to greater changes as you learn just how much improvement you can bring about without your subconscious rejecting your efforts. When you see your mate's line and observe an upcoming area of friction or mutual discomfort, then change your line to a different elevation, intensity or direction in order to offset the potential conflict.

This is the same process as knowing ahead of time that your mate will be in a bad mood and making a conscious attempt to remain cool-headed when it happens rather than becoming emotional or angry when he shows his moodiness. The difference is that you can see it coming with much more precision and exactness than you normally would. There are many times, however, when I have seen flares in my lifeline and misinterpreted them as something else when I should have looked more closely and avoided frustration which followed.

Since you now have the ability to see both your line and that of your partner and to interject subtle changes for greater compatibility, you will notice that your sexual intimacy gradually improves. Removal of areas of mutual conflict and enhancement of harmony will allow for greater physical responses on the part of both parties.

By looking forward on the lifelines, you can enhance potential improvement in your sexual satisfaction. You can also look back on the lines to rediscover the harmony that brought you and your mate together in the first place. Look closely at flares on your line. Flares represent either excitement over something going on in your life at that time or anger. If you perceive flares of anger on either or both lines, you may well rest assured that much of your sexual interest in your partner has cooled due to this conflict. Knowing this and being able to see it on your lifeline will enable you to deal with possible suppressed resentments and old hurts before re-establishing the naturalness and openness that you and he once had. Once this is done, your relationship will take on a new freshness and intimacy.

CHAPTER 3

ANATOMICAL COMPATIBILITY

Another interesting aspect of psychic readings is that they can be employed to read anatomical capabilities of potential partners/mates. Of course, with this ability, anyone can go into a public place and look over the scenery and receive impressions of many combinations of possible interesting attributes of persons nearby. This usage could be interpreted as an invasion of privacy and is not in the usual sense what we are talking about in this context.

We are more interested in the limited use on a personal basis of this skill. For example, there is a psychic reader, who in reading clients who are interested in romantic situations, begins by describing to them the pelvic region and anatomical attributes of their new or future romantic interest. She has found that her clients who are presently in a romantic involvement have told her that the information that she is giving is quite accurate.

Of course, no reader wants to solely read only this aspect of a potential mate or lover's attributes, but it is of interest that this can be determined psychically just as we have seen in an earlier chapter that via body scan, health problems can be pin-pointed. With this information provided by psychic means, the potential partner need not know that the information has been obtained or has ever been conceptualized. There is, therefore, any possible combination of determinations that can be made via this technique. This is just an additional way of psychically determining various information about someone who is of possible romantic interest.

There was a very fascinating case in which a young lady came in for a psychic reading; and in the course of the reading, it was determined that she was most concerned about a potential suitor who appeared to be avoiding her after expressing much interest in her. Through psychic imagery, it was determined that the young man had an impotence problem and had not been able to discuss this with the young lady even though he was indeed much interested in her. This reassured the subject who had felt that she herself was lacking because she had been unable to attract this particular suitor.

In another situation, a young lady came in for a reading with a "hot-cold" suitor whom she had been involved with for some time. During the course of the reading, it was seen that the male in question was bisexual. His desire for males was blocking his commitment to a romantic involvement with the subject or any other female.

Neither of the males in the two cases had been able to honestly discuss his true condition with the female in question. With the greater clarification obtained through psychic sensitivity, both young ladies were able to make a determination as to whether they even wished to pursue the relationships at hand.

In another interesting case, an elderly female came in for a reading. In the course of the reading, it was determined that she was having marital problems and difficulties in communication with her spouse following his retirement. Also, there was a great deal of anger and hostility on his part. Via psychic impressions, it was seen that the gentleman in question had a sexual performance problem which was affecting his ability to relate to his spouse and that he had been covering it up with displays of anger and hostility and avoidance of marital sex.

When his wife heard this, she acknowledged that this might be the case and that it might be due to physical problems or medical problems; but until this time, she had not suspected that this was the root of his difficulty. The couple entered into counseling and experienced much improvement in their relationship.

In another case, a young man in his twenties who had been married two years came in for a reading. It was apparent during the reading that he was having relationship problems with his wife who apparently was suffering from a lack of libido. Through psychic perception, it was revealed that the young wife had a strong interest in other females. Being from a straitlaced and highly religious background, he had not pushed the subject of "sexual inadequacy" and lack of interest on her part. With the newly discovered information being revealed to him, he was then able to leave with a better understanding of what he wanted to do and the problems he would be facing if he continued in the relationship.

In another case, a prominent statesman came in for a reading. He was apparently having emotional problems as well as marital difficulties. He was seen as being nearly at the "end of his rope". Through psychic perception, it was seen that that this man's problem was that of an exhibitionist nature. He was in terms of the vernacular, a "flasher". His wife had no idea nor had the prominent politicians, both nationally and internationally, whom he had to deal with, but there was much guilt associated with his problem which also manifested itself during the course of the reading. This man had been unable to hold any positions in any given locations for any period of time due to fear of being "found out" in that particular location. There was, consequently, a great deal of erratic movements in his lifeline and other interests shown.

In another case, a prominent professional man came in for a reading. He asked about romantic involvement in the future;

but in every case, all that could be seen was a relationship with an elderly lady, but most decidedly of a romantic nature. All his present relationships had ended after a brief period, but the elderly lady kept manifesting herself on his lifeline and in his heart reading. After much denial, he finally admitted that he had a sexual attraction for his mother and had been aware of this his entire life. He stated that no other woman attracted him in the same way. He had covered this up and even denied it to himself out of shame and guilt, but it was seen during the course of his reading. Although he came to an understanding of the severity of his problem, he did not seek additional help and wasn't heard from again.

Another case involved a young lady. It was immediately determined that she was very unhappy and felt worthless. She was an attractive young lady who seemed to have a good figure, but the image of an exceedingly flat-chested female kept appearing. When asked about this, she acknowledged that she had always felt inadequate due to being less than generously endowed and that she had taken to wearing a padded bra and sometimes even two padded bras to compensate for her imagined inadequacies. She had felt unwomanly and admitted that this was the reason she had been unable to sustain relationships past a certain point. At this juncture, she was able to discuss her feelings regarding acceptance of her figure or possible augmentation surgery and left with a better overall feeling.

A middle-aged gentleman came in for a reading. From all outward appearances, he was normal and well adjusted, but during the reading, the opposite proved to be the case. Images involving windows and certain magazines of a voyeuristic nature proved to he forthcoming. When asked about this, he admitted that he had been a voyeur for several years; and while seemingly well adjusted on the surface, he was in fact very unhappy and tortured because of his proclivities. His family had no idea of his deviation.

One evening, a young man came in and asked specifically about any romantic involvement. During the reading, images of a young lady with a very pretty face and an almost hourglass figure came forth. He knew immediately whom I was describing and wanted to know how she felt about him. He had lost touch with her and wanted to contact her again but was reluctant to do so out of fear that she would no longer be interested in him. He stated that my description of her was "right on the money".

In another case, a young woman came in, and it was soon apparent that she was also interested in information regarding a relationship. I relayed to her what I saw, and she taped the entire reading. The next morning a young man came in for a reading also regarding a relationship. I told him what I saw. I had never seen the young man before and had no idea who he was. However, after the reading, he revealed that he was the boyfriend of the young woman who had been in the night before and taped her reading.

The young lady had gone home and played the tape for him, and he, out of curiosity, came in to see what I would tell him. He was very pleased when he received the same reading regarding their relationship that she had received.

As stated earlier, you will sometimes see many and varied images of an intimate nature. It is best not to be judgmental when such may happen. If the subject can discuss such findings or admit them, then that is fine. If there is an aversion to discuss the matter or denial, then it is best to move on and continue with the reading in other areas.

As mentioned earlier in Part I, "Techniques of Psychic Reading", as a psychic, you are not licensed to do counseling and therefore should not set yourself up as a counselor. You may give an opinion to persons consulting you in the course of the readings but never call yourself a counselor, as in many areas, this, without the proper licensing requirements having been met, could result in legal entanglements for you.

Always tastefully discuss the revelations with your client in a most professional manner, just as a professional in the medical field or related health care fields might. You can be subtle and yet specific with your client in your revelations. If your client cannot discuss this or refuses to comment on the imagery, then move on to other areas. It is most probable that after the client leaves your office, he or she will fully understand what you have described even though there may have been initial skepticism or even total denial.

A complete reading involves many areas as we have seen in Part I. If physical or sexual imagery is unpleasing to your client, then use your skills to explore more pleasing subjects. Often, the crux of your client's indecision may be explained by intimate imagery, especially if romance is the primary consideration that your client is coming in for.

One young lady who was married came in for a reading due to indecision. As usual, she did not make any pre-reading statements since I prefer not to have any information volunteered by the subject before the reading has begun. During her reading, there were noted visual images of a strong chemistry between her and a young man who turned out not to be her husband when I described him. The images specifically involved lovemaking that was quite passionate and extensive.

The young lady who appeared quite demure and modest on the surface admitted that her feelings for this young man were just as depicted and that this was the reason for her great indecision and frustration, in view of the fact that she was already married. Until this time, her true feelings for this man had been totally secret.

In seeking a psychic reader or in giving psychic readings yourself, do not purposely concentrate on readings of a sexual nature. Do not concentrate on physical or sexual imagery to the point that you are known only as a "phallic" reader because this will destroy your professionalism, but just as a doctor or psychiatrist often has to deal with problems of an intimate nature in his patients, so will the psychic. Deal with it when it comes up and know that you have the ability and skills to accurately read your client in regard to these matters.

If your readings are given professionally and tastefully, your subjects will be appreciative of the information you are giving them and in no way offended. Only if you yourself treat suggestive imagery distastefully will your subjects be embarrassed and repulsed to the point of not being able to consult you again. Also, please bear in mind that any readings that you give are always strictly confidential, and never be tempted to discuss personal information with others. Your professionalism is the key to success in this field as in any other.

CHAPTER 4

Creating the Ideal Sexual Partner and On-going Relationships

We have seen that psychic readings can be of much benefit in personal relationships and also from a health standpoint. We have seen that we can read into the future as well as the present and foresee future relationships, but also we may read into the past and learn of previous relationships. Soon you will learn how to create your own ideal relationship in just the manner in which you will benefit the most.

A friend who had attended our classes and who had much psychic ability was reading herself and saw a growth in the lower left hand side of her abdominal area and sensed a slight protuberance there. She also visualized her pelvic area and saw her uterus as being tilted backward and felt strongly that this was the case although she was having no problems at the time and had not consulted a gynecologist.

A few months later when she was in for a gynecological check-up, the doctor told her that she did have a fibroid tumor on her uterus and that it was on the left side of the abdomen.

She told the gynecologist that she had felt that she had a growth in this area, but he told her that it was not possible for her to feel it. She did distinctly sense that something was in this area. He also told her that she did have a retroverted uterus, which was what she had envisioned. She did not tell him that she had seen any of this psychically.

There was a young lady who came to the office for a reading and in so doing became acquainted with another psychic in the area who did past life readings. The young lady was curious and frankly did not believe in past lives and was not even aware of exactly what that meant. During the course of the reading, the young lady had a life described to her from another century. The details were quite astounding and the events were else quite astounding because all of this had been seen by the young lady months earlier while she was under hypnosis, but the psychic had no way of knowing any of this. She had never seen the young lady before and knew nothing about her. This intrigued the young lady and she wanted the psychic to tell her as much as possible.

The psychic went on to tell the young lady that there was a man who had been with her in the previous life whom the young lady had also seen herself while under hypnosis and that he was present in her current life. The young lady, too, had seen this, while under hypnosis, but she had not been able to accept this until the psychic confirmed it. She was instructed by the psychic to contact the young man, which she did. Under hypnosis, he verified that he was indeed the same young man that had been present during the young girl's previous life in the past century.

All of this fit because the two young people were very compatible in the present life and had been friends for a long time although they had lost touch with each other in the past few years. The young lady stated that even before all of this had been revealed to her, she had felt a special closeness to the young man and had felt as if she had known him all her life and that they were soul-mates. He stated that he had felt the same way about her. There were complicating factors which worked to keep them apart in the present; but they, nevertheless, expressed the feelings that would have been expected under the circumstances. They both expressed a desire to be together in the future.

I have lost contact with the couple, but feel that if they can overcome the difficulties in the present that are separating them, they will indeed be together in the future. Their past lives as well as that of the present and future were accurately read by the psychic reader.

As we have seen, we may all change our future readings if we so desire. We still have free rein on our actions, and the course of events can be altered in some cases. There are some cases, however, where I feel that the course of events may not possibly be altered.

As we read earlier, the psychic reader could not stop the death of the man suffering from AIDS. He was able to buy him another few days or so, perhaps. However, with good intent, it never hurts to try to bring about the best happenings for others and ourselves as well. If this can be done psychically, then we have used our power or ability in a way that is beneficial and desirable for all. Even the best psychics may not be 100% accurate all the time. It is, nevertheless, the times when we are accurate that keep everything interesting.

Along these lines, we must determine how best to create the ideal sexual partner and an on-going relationship. Your ultimate goal is to obtain the Alpha state of mind, thereby allowing manifestations of the Alpha state. Begin to relax the body and focus the mind. Once the body is deeply relaxed, you can then exert total concentration on your imagery and imprint it within your subconscious mind or that of your subject.

I begin with the procedures as follows: place yourself or your subject in a quiet room in a comfortable chair, but not too comfortable. Have your subject close his or her eves and totally relax. First, relax all the muscles in the top of the head and all the muscles in the forehead, all the muscles in the cheeks and the lower jaws. Relax all the muscles in the right shoulder, the right arm all the way down to the hand. Now relax all the muscles in the left shoulder, the left arm and all the way down to the hand.

Now, have your subject relax the muscles in the chest area, breathe deeply, inhaling relaxation, exhaling all worries and stress. Inhale again deeply, let all the stress flow out. Continue the hypnotic induction as follows: "You are now totally relaxed, your chest feels so relaxed. Now relax the muscles in your abdomen, now tighten them very, very tight and relax. Let all the muscles be totally loose, limp and relaxed. Relax all the muscles in your left thigh all the way down to your calf and on down to your left foot. Let all the muscles become loose, limp and relaxed. Now relax all the muscles in your right thigh all the way down to your calf and on down to your right foot.

"Your whole body is now totally loose, limp, and relaxed. You have never felt so good, so relaxed. There is nothing that can cause you any worry now, there is no tension in your body. You now feel completely free; you are free.

"Now that your body is totally relaxed, focus your mind on the mate or lover that you desire. Visualize yourself with this person in the type of romantic, loving situation that you desire. Visualize yourself with this type person in the setting you desire, the type home or apartment and the locale you wish to live in.

"Visualize your happiness as you and your mate move forward together in the activities that you enjoy. If you desire children, visualize them in your lives. Visualize financial success, good health, vitality, love, confidence, peace, warmth, energy, optimism, hope, abundance, enthusiasm, endurance, and comfort.

"As you entertain images of your particular desires, imagine that golden rays of love and protection are entering your nostrils and are filling your lungs and are circulating throughout your body with healing and purity. See them circulating through your blood and cleansing it and cleaning your vessels. Imagine the rays healing your entire vessel and purifying your body. You are well and whole; your mate and you are as one. You will enjoy the good parts of your life, and they will make you stronger. You will forget the bad parts and any fear, and this will no longer hurt you in any way. Your heart is whole, your body is whole, and your life is whole. You have a good relationship; you will only have to think about the beauty and love in your lifestyle and the special feelings will always be with you, giving you a special feeling of comfort and warmth. Gone is any pain, fear, or unpleasantness.

"You are strong, healthy, and well, feeling better and better, with renewed enthusiasm and happiness, optimism and hope. With a love that is satisfying and rewarding, filling your life with all the things that you desire. Emotionally and physically, you are at one with yourself. You have the power to make your life exactly what you desire. You are no longer held back by any memories or associations from the past. That is all gone. You are moving ahead with renewed energy, confidence and healthiness.

"Inhale deeply, exhale and push out all old thoughts of negativity, fear and pain. Any past shortcomings will no longer bother you. Inhale new thoughts of comfort, warmth, energy, healthiness, happiness, optimism, hope, success, wealth, and abundance. You are strong now in your love. You will move forward assured in your belief in yourself and in those you love. You are restored. You will now move forward free from the bonds and shackles of the past. You are strong and successful; you are loved; you are wanted; you are appreciated. You have a strong body, a happy body, and a strong and confident mind. You are filled with thoughts of loving and being loved.

"Now count from one to five, and you will come awake. You will remember all the pleasantness and love that you have experienced, you will move ahead and bring this about in your life. You now know that you have the inner power and are now free to make your life what you want it to be.

"One, you are becoming awake. Two, more and more awake. Three, waking up now, waking up now. Four, almost awake. Five, wide-awake now, wide awake. Open your eyes now and enjoy your new-found strength and awareness" (End of hypnotic induction).

With this proper relaxation technique and the positive visualizations, either you or your subject can achieve the proper frame of mind and will be able to totally relax and focus on the proper visualization techniques. By projecting these thoughts ahead into the future, you may see the realization of your innermost desires.

To create the ideal mate for either yourself or your subject, put either of you back into the relaxation as experienced earlier. Now have your subject look ahead into the future and see himself or herself with the person of his/her dreams in the setting that he or she desires. Keep repeating this anytime that you need reassurance. You need to be as exact as you can and as detailed in your imagery as you possibly can visualize it.

Mentally visualize yourself wanting your mate/lover more than anyone else you have ever desired. Visualize your lover wanting you more than any lover at any time in the past. Your eyes will meet; your lips will meet. Your hands are moving freely and rapidly, with abandon over his/her body. See your kisses as being intent and deeply moving. You are now releasing the fabric that binds and constricts your bodies so that your bodies are now totally unrestrained and free to move together in abandon. Your lips are free to travel over the glorious expanse of your lover's body and to freely explore all the depths and secret places while your lover's lips are moving over your body in a sustained and tender caress.

Now visualize your bodies as being one, as if there is no other time or place. You are together in an eternal embrace that is sustained and more pleasurable than any previous pleasures that you have ever experienced; you are totally lost in the moment and in your love.

If there is no one in your life at present, you know now that you have the power and the confidence to bring about a happy, successful relationship with the person you desire. If there is a particular person that you wish to have a relationship with, visualize this person and picture yourselves together. However, this may not necessarily be the person you will ultimately become one with, because there may he another more compatible person with whom you will find and achieve happiness. The person is out there; you just have to adopt the proper mind frame and reach out to this person.

In this context, it is similar to looking for a home to buy. You may see many different houses and think that each of many in the same price range and with similar features is the one house for you and the only house, only to find that this particular house does not work out for you. However, later on, you find another house that you like even better and that meets your needs and desires even more. This other house was waiting for you all along, but you had to find it after seeing many others along the way.

It is sometimes the same with a future lover/mate. We may be picturing the person we want, we may be psychically creating the person we want. We also may have some frustrations when we think that we have failed to establish a relationship with a particular person, only to discover later that particular person was not right for us anyway and that there is someone else who is better and fits our psychic projections better. We did not know this and could not know this, but our subconscious knew it all along. So do not give up if you think that you have failed to achieve the particular person you want.

I know of a case where a young lady went to a psychic for a reading and then another and another and so on until she had consulted perhaps eight to ten psychics. Each of them described a young man that she was to become involved with. She thought she knew who they were talking about, but she could make no progress in a relationship with this young man. She was frustrated. She was told that this most likely was a new person, but she tried to make the description fit a man that she already knew. And, in truth, there were many similarities.

After months of frustration, emotional ups and downs, psychic reading after psychic reading, she did indeed meet another young man. However, he had all the positive characteristics of the first that she had felt that she wanted so badly but without some of the negative traits that the first young man had had. This second man did indeed fit her wants and desires much better and was in fact much more compatible with her than the first would have been. When she stopped trying to force the issue and allowed her subconscious imagery to manifest, she was fulfilled in her quest.

She is now truly happy and convinced that all one need do is relax and utilize the proper visualization techniques. Once this has been done and the mind has focused, the future projection will bring the anticipation and realization of that which is being sought, whether it be a relationship or culmination in some other area.

Another lady visualized a dream home in the mountains. She began to look for land to buy to begin construction of her mountain home. As she looked and explored many mountain lots and building sites, she made arrangement to purchase a lot that seemed to offer what she truly wanted. However, on the day of purchase, the seller changed the figures just as she was about to write out a check. She felt uneasy about this new development and decided to wait a few days before closing the deal.

While thinking about the new price differential that the seller had interjected into the deal, the lady discovered an entirely new area with twenty four-hour security, many amenities and an ideal lot for less money than the first lot. She bought the lot and built her dream home.

Many times, we will be searching for the fulfillment of our visualized imagery and will try to achieve the realization in our own way. However, the subconscious will often block our path and we will seemingly come up against many obstacles. However, the subconscious is only carrying out your orders and will continue to block out goals that are not imagery you implanted. Only with the parameters of your visual goals will your subconscious allow you to continue.

You can use this for cars, business success, places, etc. The power of the inner mind does truly lie within each of us. Each of us has for the most part untapped psychic abilities that we have yet to utilize. Once we have mastered the techniques, we can visualize and bring about untold blessings.

One young man used this technique in order to assist a friend in obtaining a wife. He was rooming with a friend of many years when the friend became much concerned with finding a suitable wife and settling down to married life. The young man visualized an ideal mate for his friend and continued to do this for some time.

Within thirty days of attempting to help his friend find a wife, the young man himself met the lady of his dreams, married and settled down within a short time thereafter.

Remember that much of what you visualize for others will also manifest in your own life. It is imperative that you entertain only good, positive, uplifting and beneficial imagery. In so doing, you will open your own subconscious up to exactly what you are creating for others. This ability is awesome. Be certain of your goals, intentions and motivations before taking action on them.

CHAPTER 5

Psychic Sex Persuasion

For the skilled person utilizing psychic abilities, there are many possibilities concerning what can be creatively achieved with the mind. We have found that in meeting a new and potential partner/lover, we are able via body scan to do a health reading on this potential mate. After having done the health reading and having assured ourselves that this is indeed a desirable and healthy person to pursue, we would also like to be able to influence our potential sex partners in the way of greatest benefit to us.

Along this line, we can visualize through the technique described in Part I, "Techniques for Psychic Reading", our intended's lifeline, and we can creatively change the lifeline to be the way we desire, i.e., give it a more upward turn, a whiter, purer cast and a less turbulent continuity. We can also picture in the future or the near future, ourselves on this person's lifeline and in the person's heart image in the frame on the wall. We can visualize this person looking toward us with a loving, appreciative glance and filling up the space in the heart frame picture as well as ourselves looking toward the potential mate with love and adoration.

This is mental posturing, which we referred to at great extent in Part 1. We can visualize ourselves with this desirable person in an intimate setting being very romantic and loving. We can even visualize ourselves in the type of romantic setting that we desire. We can visualize other elements on our own lifeline and that of our potential lover/mate. We can visualize mutual interests such as a wedding, a future home, children, going hand in hand together, and with both lifelines parallel. We can visualize the two of us moving together on the lifeline at all stages in the future. Once these thoughts and mental posturings have entered into our consciousness, we are well on our way toward our goal.

If there is no one who is a desirable mate/lover at the present time, we may also via mental posturing and lifeline imprints create a proper picture putting the desired mate/lover into it. We can place this person on our lifeline at some point in the future. We can go into visualization of this person with us at important events in the future.

In exercising psychic abilities along this line, it is for the most part best not to mention to the desired potential lover or mate that he/she is being psychically persuaded. In many cases, this might have the reverse effect, especially in the case of someone who is not familiar with psychic procedures and is perhaps even afraid of the "power".

Isn't it always nice anyway when anyone falls in love for the other person to feel that he or she has made his own decision and that there was no coercion or persuasion, no matter how gentle? To impress a future loved one with sincerity and genuine caring is always the best course. However, if one is able to gain some insights via psychic abilities or is able to bring about and achieve what he or she has desired psychically, so much the better. In some cases one may not ever know whether he or she has obtained the love and devotion of the future intended through psychic ability or his own desirable qualities; and in actuality, it does not matter if the end result is the same.

Has not each of us at some time visualized something or someone that would be desirable without particularly feeling that this person or thing would ever materialize in our lives? Then one day, maybe even years later, we come upon the very thing or person that we have been wanting for a long time? This is somewhat the way having the proper mind set for psychic persuasion works.

We must first visualize clearly what it is that we are seeking and then give some thought to how we might obtain it. In the case of relationships, we can visualize the desired mate/lover in the heart frame picture on the wall as previously mentioned whether we actually know this person or not. We can visualize our lives being financially enriched by surrounding our lifeline with green. If we are spiritual, we can visualize forces along the lifeline such as guides or protectors.

In the visualizing process for future relationships with a given person, if we see blackness along the line regarding the intended, it is best to move away from that person. Yellowness, as we have seen, may indicate tiredness, legal or illegal drug usage, or illness. Redness along the line or all the way behind the line may indicate a very serious pervasive illness such as AIDS or cancer that is life threatening. A lifeline that plunges downhill without moving back upward may indicate an imminent death.

We may try in each of these cases to help the potential mate or lover, if we choose, by trying to insert more positive imprints on the life line through mental posturing if we are already close to such a person. However, in a stranger whom we are not yet close to, signs such as the above may be taken as a "red flag" warning us to move on.

Through the usage of the above, we may indeed make our assumptions a reality. This is not to say that if someone is a very spiritual person that he or she should not practice psychic techniques. Only if there is an attempt to use the techniques for dark or satanic purposes, is there any conflict with possible spiritual beliefs. This is not to say that a psychic must or must not be spiritual. As in the general population, there are varying degrees of commitment to spirituality among psychics.

We believe that by using psychic impressions for the potential achievement and accomplishment of long desired and worthwhile goals, only good things can be obtained. As a matter of fact, the more you contemplate the awesome potential that is available to use through psychic perceptions and creative abilities, the greater will be your ability to achieve this type of consciousness for the greater good of mankind.

We have seen that by using psychic perception, we note that certain persons exhibit various spiritual beams or rays along their lifeline (sometimes in the past and sometimes in the future). We have also seen that we may see some things and possibly not others. In regarding other persons on a one-to-one basis, it is best to be honest with the subject and tell him or her what is seen as long as it is not an imminent death or something so horrifying that the subject would be severely traumatized as a result.

We have also seen that in reading persons who are unaware that we are reading them and considering them as potential mates or lovers, we should not announce that we are using psychic power, unless we know for a fact that the person would be receptive to the information. Just as we do not always tell others who are close to us our innermost thoughts, just so we should not necessarily reveal to potential mates/lovers what we have been able to see or foresee psychically.

Such announcements could very well, as stated earlier, send your potential mate/lover off in another direction where he or she is free of such "forces". With the skills, when properly utilized, however, we do have vast potential for obtaining insight into our relationships, both in the present and possibly in the future. We may use the techniques as a viable means of making our assumptions a reality.

An interesting case along this line comes to mind. A friend who has developed into quite a good psychic was unhappily without a relationship in her life. She laughingly referred to herself as being "in between men". She was a relatively quiet and seemingly demure young lady who was unable to get out very much to meet men and was quite adamant about not doing the bar scene.

She has stated quite often that she would never meet a new man in her present job due to long hours and no social activity. However, she began to visualize on her lifeline a handsome man of a description that met her innermost desires. She also visualized a meeting of her and this man, his immediate attraction to her and her subsequent attraction to him. She visualized a soul-mate type of feeling between them. She went further into it and visualized all of the characteristics that she truly wanted in a man, as she jokingly would say that she had been married twice and not found what she wanted yet. She visualized an ideal wedding situation followed by their moving into a gorgeous home in a location that held great interest for her.

Some time elapsed and this woman had made no changes in her lifestyle other than she was more active and getting out more. It was a few months after this time that she called me to relate that she had indeed found the man of her dreams, that they were planning a wedding of the type she had described and that they would be shortly moving into a fine new home.

Now many will entertain the question: Was this manifestation a result of the woman's visualization or was the woman's visualization actually brought about because of the manifestation that was to be forthcoming? Skeptics would say probably that this was all coincidence. In truth, perhaps the woman's getting out more because she had visualized all of this psychically and because she was more "open and receptive" to this particular manifestation caused it to come about. Or perhaps it was indeed there all the time and all the woman had to do was tune into it. Who can say for certain? However, it did work out very well in her case and with her psychic abilities being extensive, I feel that it is highly possible that she was able to bring about that which she desired. She herself said that she had never tried anything like this before and had never had the real faith to believe that it could transpire. Now, however, she is firmly convinced that what we can see mentally can become reality.

Another interesting note to this case is that soon after she started visualizing this scenario, other psychics gave her readings. Each psychic described the same identical scene that she had seen in her mind, and all of them told her that this would come to pass.

Another case which clearly will illustrate just how much a mental picture will influence your personal relationships concerns a young lady who was studying for a new career in hypnotherapy. She related that she was a very visual person and for some time had mentally entertained a story line in her mind that showed her entering into a relationship with a new man who would fall in love with her. The relationship would move on, and then she would visualize him leaving her, going to another woman and then returning to her. She said that she thought nothing of the mental movie in her mind, but one day she suddenly awakened to find that her life with each new man was going just exactly like the negative mental images she had created.

She changed her mental images, and her life took a new direction; and her latest romance has been lasting, with no interest on the part of her partner to seek other women. She stated that she "astounded" herself when she finally realized that she had been creating her own problems and then knew that she could also create her own solutions.

CHAPTER 6

DREAM SEX—ASTRAL SEX

Dreams are referred to as "day residue". This means that most of our dreams are brought about by events or stimulation in our day to day lives that become symbolized by the subconscious in the form of dream images. Bodily needs, tensions, unreleased sexual frustrations and other emotionally charged situations are often released through dream imagery.

Everyone dreams but some people do not remember much about their dreams, only fragments which are quickly forgotten if not written down. However, sex dreams occur from time to time during one's life and are usually remembered in varying degrees of detail.

If you wish to stimulate specific dreams for your own entertainment, you can learn to program yourself to dream what you wish to dream. Simply repeat to yourself in a repetitious manner that "Tonight I will dream about making love. It will be wonderful, fulfilling and vibrant. I will fully remember my dream when I wake up in the morning." Repeat this over and over just before you drift off to sleep and, with practice, you will begin to realize more frequent sex dreams and be able to remember them better than you ever have in the past.

You can also program yourself for psychic dreams in which you tell yourself that you will dream of someone who will be your future lover/mate. Continue to do this with constant regularity and your subconscious will answer you with vivid images and impressions. The more exact your request, the clearer will be your dream. Program yourself for success, wealth, romance, adventure and another type of need that you may have. Your mind will respond accordingly, and you will begin to have dreams of a very informative or revealing nature in total accord with what you have programmed into it.

When you begin to remember more of your dreams, write them down, and you will notice that the content of the dreams will become clearer as you move along. This will take practice and patience but can well be worth your while.

Lucid dreaming is a whole new ball game. Lucid dreaming is waking up in the dream and becoming aware that you are indeed dreaming. You continue to dream while awake in the dream itself and actually can direct the dream and make it do or show you anything you want, including vivid sexual experiences, romantic encounters, cartoon involvement, psychedelic experiences or facing dragons or personal fears.

Lucid dreaming has been used in therapy in order to enable the patient to deal with his problem at the subconscious level, to solve problems which were frustrating him and just for general personal entertainment. The lucid dream is vivid and real, and your consciousness will become totally engrossed in the dream just as though you were actually doing whatever you are dreaming.

There is a technique that will enable you to enter your subconscious mind and command your dreams while still conscious. As you have learned earlier, you can relax yourself to the point where your body is totally relaxed and your mind can be focused to total concentration on one idea or thought.

Visualize your hands to be right in front of your face and then picture them moving away from your face and expanding outward in a "welcoming" gesture as though inviting you to follow them outward and into the dream scene itself. As you do this, visualize a scene in your mind and then visualize yourself walking out into that scene. Once you have done this, continue to visualize the scene with trees, houses, specific locations, etc., until you know that you have become a part of the pictured scene. Once you become a part of the scene, mentally command an image to come forth and actively participate with this image until you are ready for another scene.

I knew a student who entered into the dream state and saw Disney characters. He walked and talked with Mickey Mouse, Donald Duck, and many other characters. He and Mickey went for a drive in Mickey's cartoon car. However, he was somewhat embarrassed by such a juvenile dream experience, and he was reluctant to re-enter the dream world again on a conscious basis.

For seeking a future relationship, however, lucid dreaming can be a tremendous tool. It takes about three weeks of constant practice to enable you to enter the dream state at will; but once you do, you can bring forth any type of experience or relationship that you desire.

Once you have entered the dream state and are not so awed at your ability, it is then time to begin serious dream manipulation for your own advancement. You can start with yourself in the dream walking into your future and arriving at certain stations along the way and bringing into actual being the events you wish to happen in your life. The method is much like the lifeline visualization methods taught earlier in the book, but in the dream state it is totally real to you. As long as you remain in this state, you will actually feel as though these things are happening to you in a totally experiential way.

When you visualize your lifeline and place people or events on it in your creative fashion for the future, you can actually touch it, feel it and experience it in the lucid dream state. However, this state is fickle and short-lived. You may be able to sustain it only for a few seconds to possibly a few minutes. Some people can sustain it longer, but it takes much practice.

Astral travel is a phenomenon that very few people have experienced but one in which many thousands would like to experience. It involves your inner self actually leaving your physical body and moving around just as though you were in the body but with notable exceptions.

If you ever are able to get out of your body, you will experience being able to go through doors or walls without restraint. You can see, hear and experience things, but material items or objects will not stop you from doing what you want. You can soar to great heights, fly to distant places and visit friends or loved ones, only they will not know that you are there.

I have had this experience only once, and it was only a partial leaving of the body. I was awakened one night with a loud humming in my head. As I awakened to find out what the noise was, I became aware that I was halfway out of my body and a bright light was shining from me and lighting the room. Everything was visible even though it was during the dark of night. I knew what was happening and very much wanted it to continue but was afraid at the same time. I stopped moving out from the body and gradually re-entered the body and the humming ceased.

The technique for astral travel is to relax your body with your face upward on a bed or the floor. Close your eyes and visualize a long body just above your physical body and see it connected to the physical by a white cord to your forehead. As you see the image above you, imagine that you are gradually ascending into the form above you. When you have done this, you will have allowed your consciousness to become detached from your body.

When you have achieved this ability, you can travel anywhere you want to go and experience many things other than just the physical. You can walk about, visit others who are also in the astral plane and, yes, encounter relationships as well.

I have read about sexual experiences among persons who are engaged in astral travel. They relate that it is totally fulfilling and that you and your mate are one to a degree that the physical can never know. I have only read of this and do not know, personally, of anyone who has done so. However, it is worth mentioning for your exploration.

CHAPTER 7

How to Recognize and Avoid Sexual Abnormals

We have all read horror stories involving leaving a child with a babysitter who either molested the child or caused even greater harm. We have heard or read about the Boy Scout leader who enticed young boys into sexual acts and the priests and religious leaders who have done the same. Also, what woman wants to marry a homosexual man? No college student wants to be raped or harmed by a campus rapist or murdered by some maniac. How can we protect ourselves and our loved ones from such disasters? Is protection even possible?

If you have a daughter in college and want to give her the optimum protection you possibly can, then give her future a reading and open your conscious awareness for the unthinkable. Instead of trying to look for only the good, open up and see if you observe any type of negativity surrounding her at any given point along her lifeline. See if you can visualize the lifeline and notice any abnormality or disruption of the line. If so, continue to view the scene and discover what may be causing the disturbance on the line. It may be only school worries or a dispute with her regular boyfriend. However, violence will show in different ways on a lifeline. You may see large flares in the line, redness in the line if there is blood involved or hear screaming if there is terror or attack ahead.

This is the type of material that no parent can easily tune in to, and it may well be better for both the parent and the child that a good psychic be consulted rather than someone close. However, if you can be objective and look with the intent of being able to ward off tragedy before it happens, then you are far the better for it. If you do see possible trouble for a loved one in the future, clear the image and begin constructive recreation of the lifeline. Where you see an abnormality, replace it with a normal lifeline, healthy, clear and vibrant. Visualize a clear shield surrounding and protecting the lifeline of your loved one. Picture this line as being protected from all harm. See the person, place, or thing that may cause the harm as being far away and unable to reach your loved one at any time. If you work with your daughter or other loved one and he or she cooperates with you in visualizing the same protection surrounding the lifeline, your results will be much better. Do what you have to do to protect the life of your loved one. However, exert caution in that you do not terrify your child or loved one by describing potentially gruesome future scenarios. It is best to work to provide protection but not to instill fear.

It has been my experience that your children will tend to cooperate with you and help you along with your image projection once you have explained just what you see and ask for their help. If you see a problem on a Thursday when some scheduled activity is due, change the activity if possible, and replace the entire day to avoid totally the prior schedule. Sometimes this is impossible, but your child can be aware of possible situations and make mental adjustments and take extra precautions to avoid the type of problems which may be precipitated in that day or during a set time or event.

Can you actually change the future by becoming aware of what is going to happen and then changing your actions to counter what you have seen? The answer to that question is "yes". If you have the vision to see imminent danger, you also have the common sense to avoid the area of indicated danger. If you meet someone and sense something negative, then you should avoid this person. If you continue to associate with him and something unpleasant happens, who is to blame?

When you schedule a babysitter for your children, mentally visualize the entire evening. See him or her with the sitter and notice if you see, hear or feel any negativity or disturbance of any kind. If you feel calm, secure and assured that the evening will go well, then employ the sitter and be on your way. However, any unusual disturbances or dark images may warrant calling another person to sit with your children.

The same applies with dating. If you meet someone and sense that there is more than meets the eye in a negative sense, you probably should move on. What you are picking up may well be sexually abnormal habits, hidden anger, repressions or any number of subsurface problems. You have the talent — use it!

Many psychics are used for criminal investigations to help solve crimes. How much more wonderful it is to prevent crimes than have to solve them after the fact. Had Abraham Lincoln heeded psychic warnings before going to Ford's theater, history might have been different. John Kennedy may well have finished out his term if he had heeded psychic warnings not to go to Dallas.

There have been numerous cases when people were about to board a plane and suddenly felt cold or fearful and refused to take that particular plane only to discover that it crashed on the very flight they were to have taken. There have been many cases of people changing trip plans, refusing to enter certain elevators, postponing surgery, avoiding speaking engagement, etc., and later finding out that the event that they had originally planned would have been a catastrophe had they gone ahead with original plans.

Listen to your inner voice. Practice these techniques and you will be able to help not only yourself, but others as well. When you give a reading and are tuned in to your subject's romantic interest, focus your attention on the subject's object of affection. Notice whether or not that person has encountered any sexual incidents involving someone of the same sex. Notice if he or she has engaged in any perverse or kinky sex acts in the past and see if you can see any type of pattern in the line. When you become practiced in readings, you will be able to recognize sexual aberrations and inherent problems and be able to warn your client of impending disaster. You will also be able to see true, loving and normal physical affection traits, which would give the green light to your client to pursue this relationship and expect good things.

When you read homosexuals, you will be able to see the partner in question and whether or not that partner is truly interested in your client or if his mind is on other people. You can tell the intensity of the relationship, duration of the encounter and about how much longer the relationship will last. You may well take a look at your subject, also, as the past habits of your client will affect the future of the proposed relationship.

If you are reading a homosexual or heterosexual male or female, the main concern for new relationships will be diseases and/or infections. We have already discussed psychic perception in this area, and you may want to review that particular section. After that comes the sincerity or romantic interest that the other partner may or may not have. Once these two areas are cleared, you may move on to other things of interest to your client.

Remember the technique is to visualize the future lifeline of your loved one. Check to see if there are any problematic areas. If there are troublesome areas in the line, use creative visualization to correct the situation and add a halo of protection around the line. If you will use this method and obtain the cooperation of your loved one, you will be able to avoid many problems that otherwise would have occurred.

For example, a friend of ours who has been an active psychic for years used her psychic abilities to protect her from an imminent danger. She has been recently divorced and had just started back dating. She was out on a date with a young man whom she had known for many years, but had never dated before.

Toward the end of the evening, they went back to his apartment; and due to the fact that they had known each other for a long time and were also strongly attracted to each other, they were soon in an intimate embrace and near the point of having sex. The man had told her that he had recently had a STD but had taken medication and was all right at that time. The young lady believed him, but there was a feeling that something was not right and she was vacillating about having actual intercourse with him. She did not have any contraceptives and neither did he, but she was very tempted and he was being very persuasive. It was at this point that she saw a vision of something dark over his right shoulder. It was like there was a dark negative force surrounding him

She immediately took this to mean that she should beware getting involved with the man, and she left the apartment. She didn't see him for several years after this but ran into him one day later through mutual friends. During the course of the conversation, he alluded to the last time they had been together. Then he mentioned to her that he had been sick for about two years after that time with a recurrence of STD and that it was good that she did not have sex with him. She was surprised by his candor but appreciated very much the fact that her own psychic abilities had led her away from danger.

SUMMARY

From the guidelines and techniques outlined in Part I, "Techniques of Psychic Reading", we have moved to direct application of our psychic techniques in areas in which we may be most interested. In Part II, we have dealt with relationships and applications of psychic sex to our present and future relationships.

As we go back over techniques, let us now recall that in initially touching the subject's hand, we can determine whether that person is a warm-hearted, extremely warm-hearted, cautious, warm with caution, or a cool individual. This will give us an indication in the very beginning as to what emotionality the future partner for this subject should possess as well in order to be compatible with the subject you are reading.

Next, when doing the body or health scan, let us remember that areas that appear "yellow" can signify chronic illness, medication or illegal drugs or simply, extreme tiredness. "Black" indicates old areas of illness and "red" indicates current, virulent, possibly very intense illness. There may also be stages in-between, such as brown areas, pink areas, with brown being less intense than black and pink less intense than red.

Also, as we picture our subject's lifeline, we may see areas around the lifeline or even on the line itself that are colored. Red, as we have seen, around the lifeline or solid in the background of the lifeline indicates very strong illness. There was a friend who was having a reading done on her boyfriend (the reading was done through her), and the psychic picked up that the background was suddenly changing to red in the future all behind his lifeline. She told the young lady that it seemed that he would be very ill sometime in the immediate future. The young lady left not really knowing what to believe, as her boyfriend was currently quite healthy, young and vital. She did not mention this to him because she did hope that the psychic was wrong.

About one month later, the young lady's boyfriend was out of town on a hunting trip; and as it turned out, he met with a near fatal accident. He lost a lot of blood and was on medication for many months thereafter plus had to eventually have surgery, with lingering after-effects for many months. The young lady remembered what the psychic had said and understood then the significance of the red background. This young lady had been a student in one of our classes and had some psychic ability herself, but had never encountered a solid red background before in a reading.

Another woman was in for a reading and her lifeline showed not a red background, but red along the lifeline in the future. She was told that she might well go to the doctor for a check-up, but she stated that she was feeling fine. As it turned out, very shortly into the future, she came down with a debilitating illness, which disabled her for about eighteen months, and was a case which the doctors were not at all sure about. She could hardly get out of bed for more than an hour or so a day although all of her medical tests checked out all right. She felt that her entire body was on the verge of a total breakdown. As much as she wanted to get up and do things, her body simply would not respond. There was no medical treatment particularly that was found to be of help, other than a mild tranquilizer.

This young lady fervently went to work on herself through meditation. She used hypnotherapy, prayer, control of her lifestyle, pacing her work, resting when she began to get tired, concentrating on more sleep and less overall stress, increased exercise and participation in enjoyable activities rather than all work-related and family-related obligations. She is now quite well and upon having a psychic reading, she shows no more evidence of the redness; and all the pinkness has now disappeared as well.

Other colors along the lifeline and around are also of special note as we have discussed. Black along the lifeline or around it may indicate something bad or possibly nefarious, not necessarily in the subject himself but perhaps in his associates or concerning some project or deal that he may be involved in. If visualized along the lifeline in the future, a future deal or happening that he may be about to become involved in may well be something to avoid. This may denote criminal activities, shady dealings of a financial nature, etc. At any rate, such indications should serve to caution that person to beware.

If you do see negativity surrounding your subject or someone that your subject is about to encounter in the future, you should be careful in revealing this to your subject. Do not say, "I see that you are an evil person, that you are into evil activities, etc." This, even if true, will repel your subject. Use your own best judgment in telling the person what you see. Subtlety is best in such cases. You may ask your subject if he or she has any upcoming business deals or projects involving other persons whom he is unsure about or if he has any associates that are involved in questionable activities or something of this nature. If this is not the case, then the subject himself may well be into undesirable activities and will know what you are alluding to even if he or she does not acknowledge it.

The color "Yellow", as we have stated, may indicate tiredness, drug usage (illegal or legal) , heavy medication or a combination of all of the above. If the lifeline is yellow all along, one or more of the above is probably the case. I was reading a lady on TV one time, and I noticed that another lifeline came into view other than hers. This line was very yellow, and I remarked about seeing the line and felt that she was very concerned about this person. The lady informed me that her mother had just been released from the hospital and was recovering from a bad illness and was very tired and on heavy medication. If the lifeline is clear, white or translucent, then everything is fine and as it should be.

If you see an erratic lifeline, then the subject is an up and down person — either emotionally or activity wise. If the lifeline is very flat, the subject has little or no interests in life and very little activity. Periods of little activity followed by activity are often shown in the lifeline as flat segments followed by wavy segments followed by flat again, etc.

If you see a lifeline going downhill, then the subject is probably depressed or sad. A lifeline that is downhill and then back up is indicative of depression. Also, a lifeline that is fairly even and then dips way down like a pothole in the road indicates depression for that particular period of time.

For example, a friend called me and was very unhappy in his job. When he hung up the phone, I saw his lifeline; and it very soon was taking a big dip, much like the Grand Canyon, but then was slowly moving back up. And, indeed, within a couple of days, the friend called me back and told me that he had been fired right after we talked on the phone and that he had no resources and nothing that he could do and he felt on the bottom. A few months later, he did obtain another position and started out of the hole, as had been seen, and back up. When I told him what I had seen, he was amazed at the accuracy.

Also, another friend was in for a reading during a classroom session and was read by another student who saw a whole field of green grass and a cow chomping it all up. The student told the lady that was being read what she had seen. The lady said that she had trouble holding on to money and all that she had seemed to get "gobbled up". Green, as we have seen earlier, signifies money on or around the lifeline.

One young man was read, and it was seen that he would be ascending stairs with green grass growing on them, about a foot high. The first step was average size, the next step was a large step up and then the next step was average again. I interpreted that to mean that he would he getting a lot of money, but in stages, an average amount in the beginning followed by a big step up and then more, but in an average increment. This was precisely what happened. The young man, who had his own business, called me and told me that his business had started to really take off, that everything had increased a pretty good bit and then it really skyrocketed and then increased even more, but pretty much steadily after that. You can easily see why green tends to signify financial increases, new jobs, and is a portent of increase and good.

We have seen that a white or golden ray along a lifeline indicates spirituality. The position on the lifeline, whether in the past currently or in the future, will tell us about the subject's spirituality — whether it is a thing of the past, a present interest or whether it will be in his or her future.

You will many times notice white sparkles along the lifeline. This, also, indicates spirituality and perhaps angels or guides in that person's life. I have read individuals that have no such sparkles. Others I have read may have from three to five sparkles. Sometimes they are blue or red in addition to white. At times the rays extend all the way along the lifeline of the subject, indicating a strong spirituality.

In giving a reading, it is best to tell your subject what you may see in reference to spirituality; but if this is contrary to your own beliefs, do not comment on it. Various individuals will come in with various degrees of spirituality.

Auras are read in much the same way that sparkles are read. It may show around your subject's head in various colors - white, blue, green, yellow, black, brown or other colors. In reading auras, as we stated before, we need to look slightly off from the person to see the impression of the aura. The colors may be interpreted according to the general color connotations that we have discussed. Since you will see more of an impression of a color rather than the actual color itself, these may vary with the individual.

One lady came in for a reading and her aura was very unbalanced.

It was stronger on one side than the other. This indicated that her life was unbalanced, perhaps either her work life or home life was out of balance. At any rate, something in her aura showed that she was neglecting something in her life that needed to be corrected.

Another example of color interpretation can be illustrated through a young man who was read and found to have a period of blackness on his lifeline in the past. He was subtly told about this and asked if he had been involved in anything funny in the past or had had any unpleasant associates. He stated that he had been a heavy drug user and had in so doing been associated with a lot of persons using drugs and also some selling drugs and that he had at times felt as if his soul was no longer his. He has been clean now for a number of years, but if the lifeline is pictured, the area of blackness is there in the past.

As stated earlier, if in considering a future business deal or a future partnership, one sees blackness or darkness around the individual involved, then that future event or dealings regarding that individual should be avoided.

Some time back I was talking with a friend of more than twenty years, when he stated that he had just made an investment in a new business venture and expected to earn a tremendous amount of money soon. As soon as he had spoken the words, I suddenly felt a heavy negativity surrounding the entire situation. I waited for him to ask me for my opinion, but he never did. He had gone ahead without consulting anyone and was very excited about the venture. After about a year, I learned that he had lost approximately $65,000.00 on the deal, and it was due to someone in the company coming in and taking over through bankruptcy, etc. I wish that my friend had sought advice before acting. I never told him of my impressions.

I have another psychic friend who states that she sometimes sees an image of the Devil or has an impression of the Devil around persons she comes into contact with. She is positive of this and feels very strongly about it. In many cases, she has received later verification that those seen with the Devil near them were involved in illegal or criminal activities.

Sometimes, the important thing is not what we see but how we interpret it, as Chapter 8 explains. If you feel "evil", see "evil", if it is black or a little devil or whatever, for you that is an indication to beware of that person or activity or at least, if you are skeptical, to further investigate that person or proposal before proceeding further.

Also, along these same lines, if a lifeline going down indicates depression or continuously down, death, then a lifeline going up will indicate that the subject is moving into a good period, that things are picking up for that person. As we have seen, some individuals may evince an up and a down lifeline all the time. In certain mental cases, this is especially true. Manic-depressive illness will often appear on the lifeline as highs and lows, but constantly. Chronic depression may appear as a downward lifeline but not stopping, as in death.

One young man was read who had a lifeline that was choppy like a block up and then a block down and a block up and a block down. His wife and his mother-in-law both confirmed that he was highly emotionally unstable, with periods of extreme niceness followed by total irrationality.

Whether these persons are truly mentally ill, you as a psychic cannot determine because you are not medically trained. It is best to leave that for the professionals; however, you may receive indications of it in the lifeline of the subject. Also, in these cases, use discretion and be subtle in telling your subject that he or she might have a serious emotional problem or a mental problem. Rather, you might say, I see periods of emotional turmoil in your life or I see some sadness or I see shifts in your feelings, highs and lows, and then see what your subject will say.

In readings involving sexual relationships, this type of reading is especially important in gaining greater knowledge of one's future partner's emotionality. The color indicators that we have described earlier may give quite a bit of information regarding a future partner.

Along these lines, a young couple came in and wanted a joint reading, which is not the usual case. However, they were concerned about compatibility for a future marriage. I saw their lifelines intersecting only at certain points, with wide distances in between the intersections, which I interpreted to mean that they had little in common and would have brief periods of togetherness if they did indeed marry. I told them that I saw them together at certain times and apart at other times, that there would be some differences.

In spite of the warning, they did marry and have since had the predicted amount of differences and periods of aloofness, to the point that they are now anticipating divorce. Always tell your subject what you see and do it in a tactful and professional manner. Do not give orders or directions, simply relate what you see as the truth and let them decide on their destiny.

Another couple sought advice from a fellow psychic regarding compatibility, and the psychic visualized a heart and it was solid except for a sector that was about 1/16 of the heart. The psychic took this to mean that they had a great deal in common and only in a very small area would they be incompatible. Another couple that she read at the same time, whom had come in with the other couple, was shown to have a heart that was missing close to one-half. This indicated to the psychic that this young couple had very little in common and would have a lot of areas of contention, if they married.

Another young lady had been involved in a serious relationship with a young man for four years and they had discussed marriage at a great length when suddenly he began to cool although he pretended that everything was all right. The young lady who was very intuitive, and now knows that she is outright psychic, at that time, felt that something was wrong but didn't know what it was. Then one night she was at home and the telephone rang, and her mother answered it. The young lady was in another room and overheard her mother who apparently was talking with her aunt say, "She doesn't care". The young lady, at that moment, took that to mean that they were talking about her and that her boyfriend was involved with another woman and was getting married. The thought just popped into her head.

When her mother hung up the phone and came back into the room, the young lady asked her mother what the call was about. Her mother told her that "John is getting married." The young lady then said, "I know he is," and her mother asked her how she could possibly know that, and she stated that she had just sensed that was what it was. She then went out to the front lawn and picked up the newspaper, knowing beforehand that the engagement would be in that evening's paper. Indeed, there in the paper was the announcement of the engagement and what was worse, the marriage was going to be held on her birthday.

Thus, we see that there are many ways in which we may use psychic readings in relationships. Psychic sex is a potentially useful and highly beneficial area in which psychic ability may be utilized to help us with present relationships and also in planning for future relationships.

As explained earlier, it is not necessary to announce to anyone that you are doing a reading if this person is a potential future partner/spouse, especially in the case of individuals who may not be familiar with psychic ability or may not even understand psychic ability and its potential. And, in reading a subject professionally, always be subtle in what is said and revealed. Use good judgment, but do not deliberately change what you see or misrepresent to your subject, even if your intentions are good.

If we follow the guidelines and techniques as outlined, we will all be far more astute and hopefully more successful in establishing the relationships that we desire and eliminating potentially unfulfilling ones, which in the final analysis is the ultimate goal for most persons.

Proper "Mind Frame" and "Thought Posture" techniques, as described herein, enable each of us to become accomplished professionals in this field. Never before have such precise and workable techniques been available anywhere in the world. Use them wisely.

APPENDIX

Images and Interpretations

The following materials are graphically reproduced images that you will see when you utilize the basic techniques for picturing the lifeline and other "settings" for psychic perception. The uses of these images are more fully explained earlier in this volume and are intended to be used solely for clarification and enhancement of techniques and procedures alluded to earlier in this volume.

Please note no psychic revelations or imagery or attempts at revelations are intended in any way to be used by anyone for medical diagnosis and/or treatment. Only a medical professional is qualified to diagnose and/or treat medical conditions; and only a licensed professional is qualified to render counseling or therapy.

Lifelines (Images and Interpretations)

Fig 1. Lifeline of a subject who is highly emotionally variable.

Fig 2. Lifeline of a subject who is placid, for the most part, with little activity or interests.

Lifelines (Images and Interpretations)

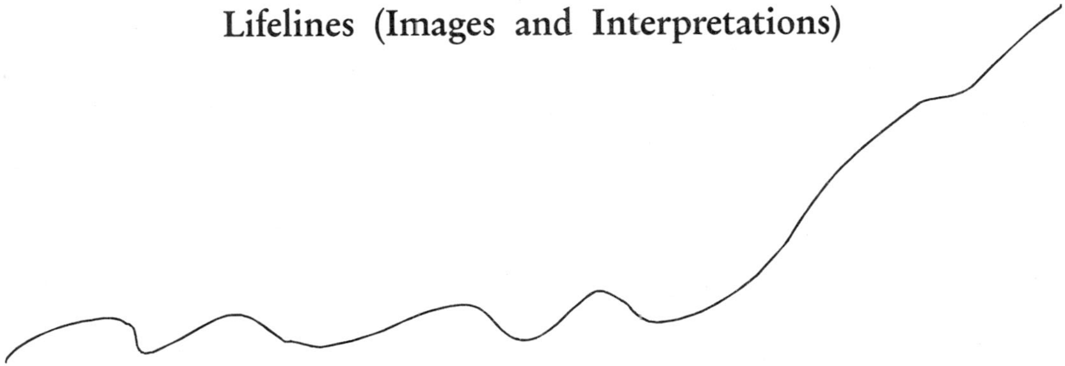

Fig 3. Lifeline of a wavering, indecisive individual for whom things will pick up tremendously.

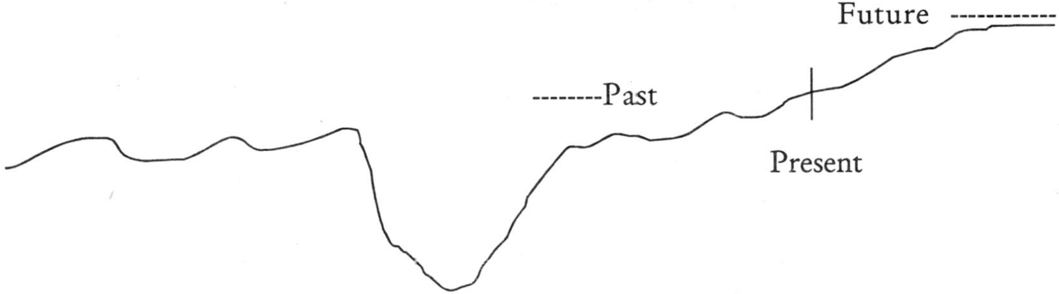

Fig 4. Lifeline of an emotionally variable but yet fairly stable individual who has experienced a large depression in the past, but has moved out of it.

Lifelines (Images and Interpretations)

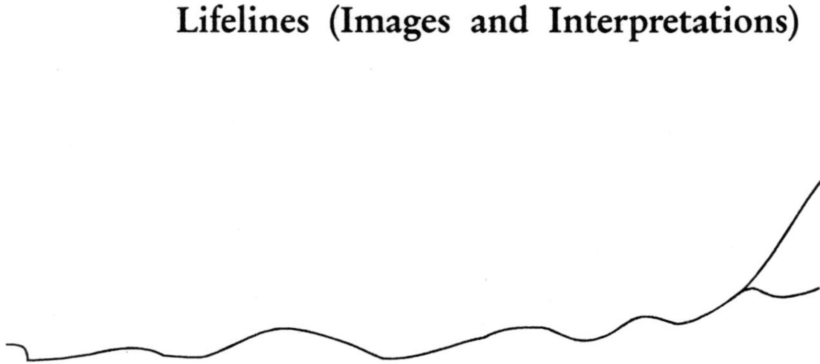

Fig 5. Diagram of a small business, continuing at a regular rate, for the most part some ups and downs, then tremendous increase with another smaller interest stopping.

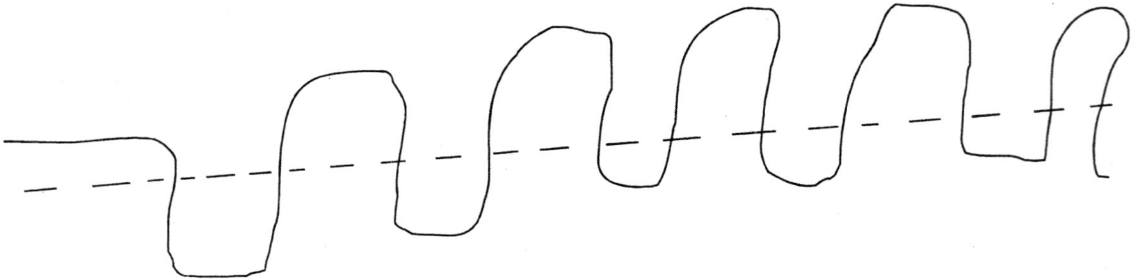

Fig 6. Lifeline of a highly emotional subject, with pronounced highs and lows. It can be seen by dissection straight across just how pronounced the highs and lows are.

Lifelines (Images and Interpretations)

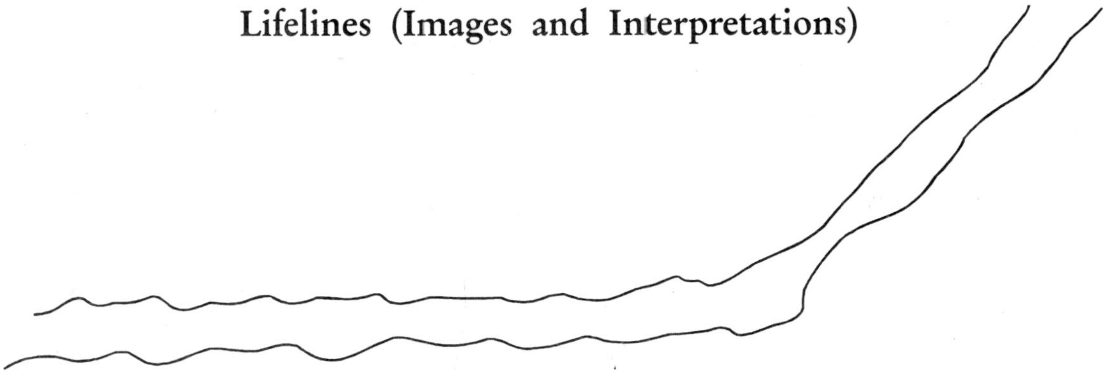

Fig 7. Lifelines of a couple, who are, for the most part, in tandem together. Increase in overall situation is mirrored by increase in partner's overall situation.

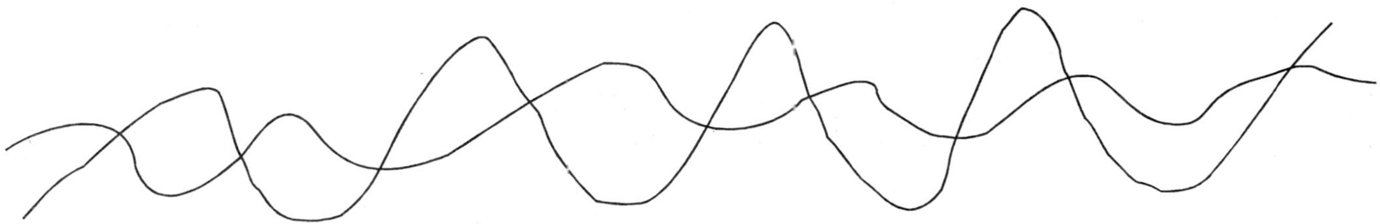

Fig 8. Lifelines of a couple, who are rarely in tandem. Lifelines intersect rarely and sporadically.

Compatibility (Images and Interpretations)

Fig 9. Couple whose relationship as evinced by the solid heart (with only a small slither or slice missing) is almost completely whole, indicating high compatibility.

Fig 10. Couple whose relationship is only about half complete as evinced by one half of the heart missing.

Lifelines (Images and Interpretations)

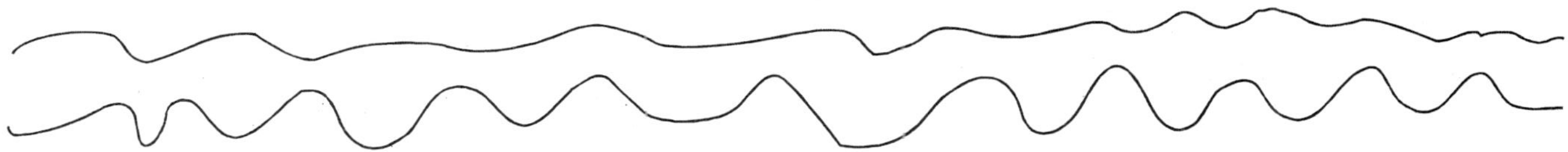

Fig 11. Lifelines of a couple with different emotional make-ups. One is more placid. The other is more prone to emotional jags.

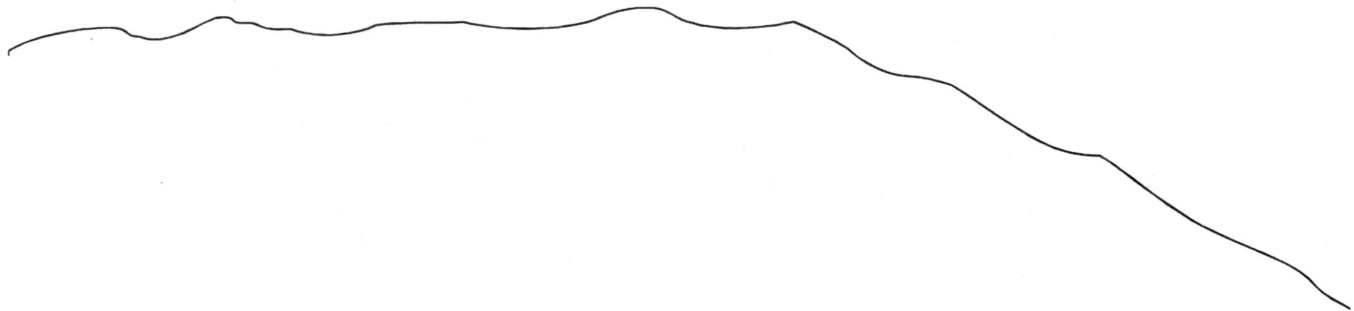

Fig 12. Diagram showing lifeline of an inactive, frail older man whose health is on the decline and actually deteriorating to the point of death in a short period of time.

Lifelines (Images and Interpretations)

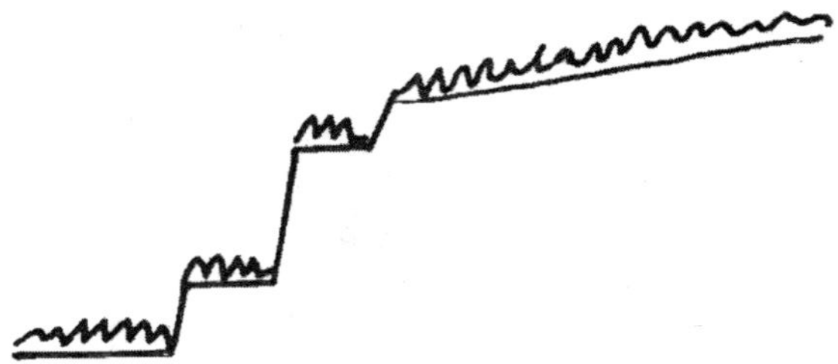

Fig 13. Lifeline showing financial increase in stair-step fashion. Squiggles represent money on stair-steps.

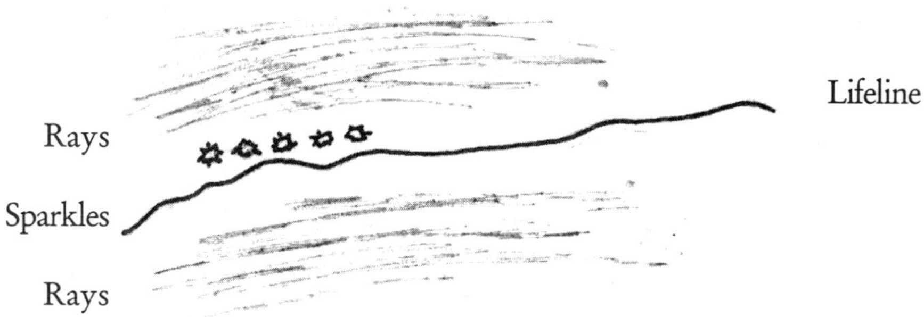

Fig 14. Lifeline showing rays of spirituality and sparkles from spirituality in the past.

Lifelines (Images and Interpretations)

Fig 15. Lifeline of a young man showing a future relationship, mutual love, a chapel and home for the couple.

Fig 16. Heart frame picture of couple showing closeness, but still some independence on both their parts.

Heart frame picture of couple who appear to be in different planes.

Lifelines (Images and Interpretations)

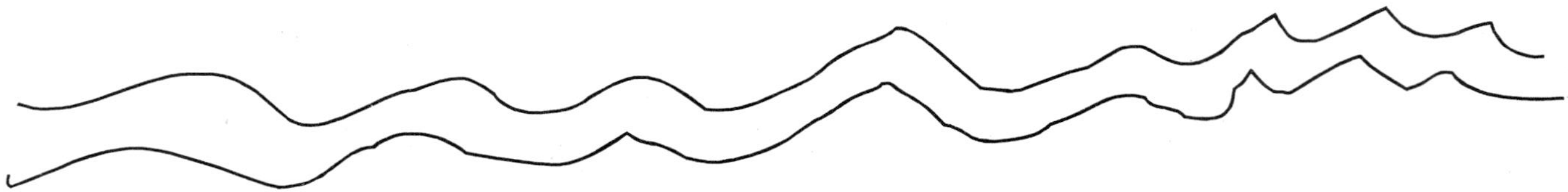

Fig 17. Diagram showing lifeline of subject without any romantic partner but having parallel lifelines due possibly to multiple personality.

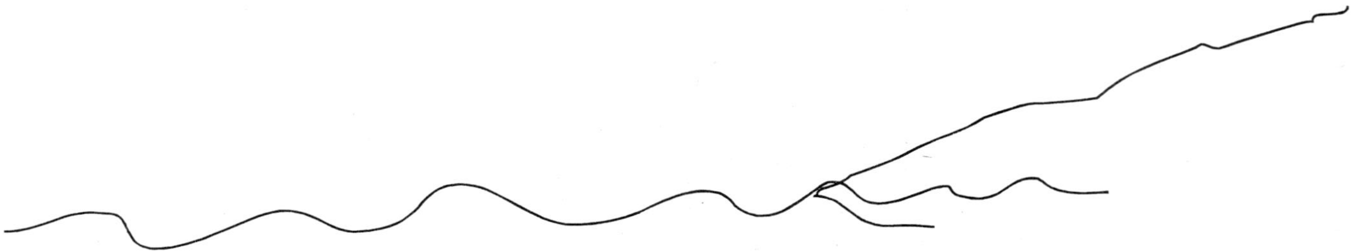

Fig 18. Lifeline of subject with three different interests, one of which is brief and ending, a second lasting somewhat longer, but a primary interest continuing onward and upward.

Lifelines (Images and Interpretations)

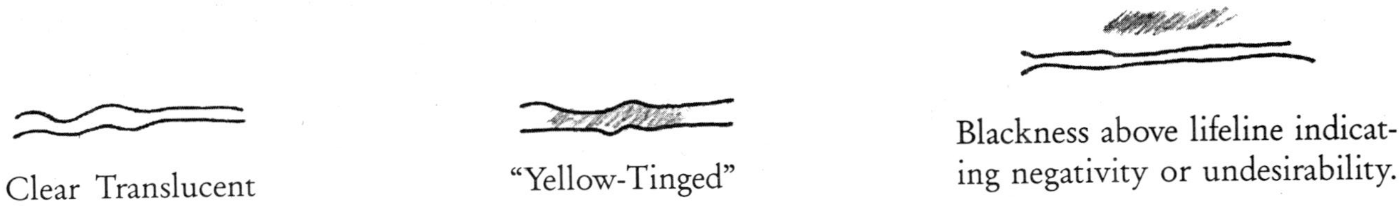

Fig 19. Diagram of outlines of lifelines shown as solid lines actually are visualized as open lines, colored either clear translucent white, yellow or with blackness or redness possibly around the lifeline.

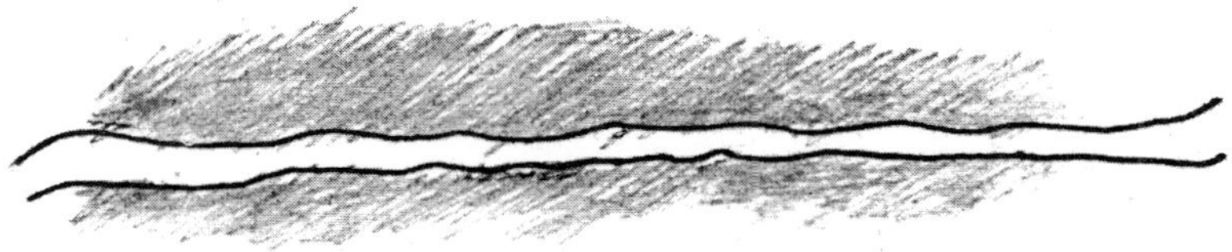

Fig 20. Solid redness all around lifeline, indicating serious, virulent illness.

Lifelines (Images and Interpretations)

Fig 21. Lifeline of a subject read through another subject, who had died from electrocution.

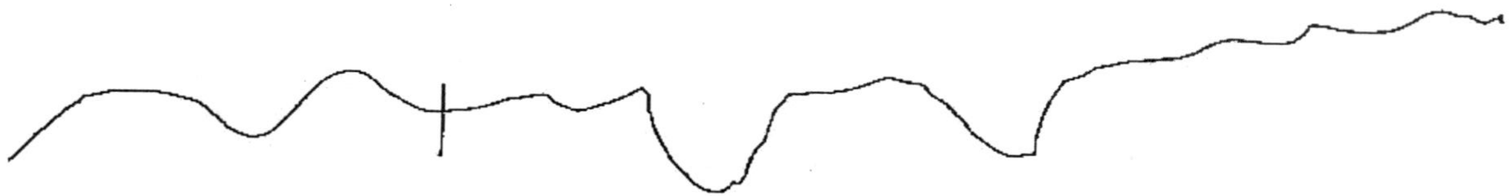

Fig 22. Lifeline of a man who is changeable and is going to have two depressed periods coming up in his life.

Images and Interpretations

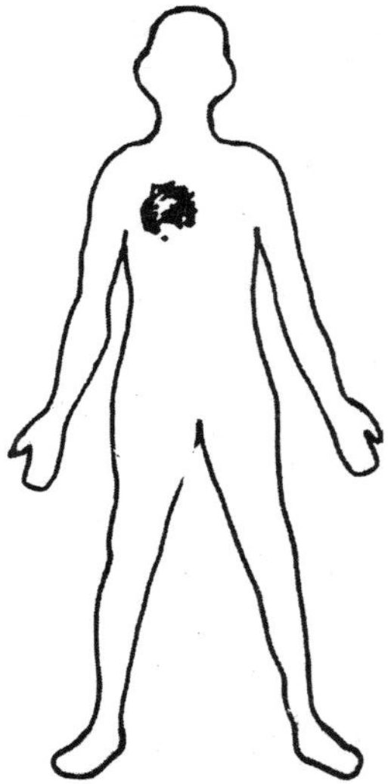

Fig 23. Body scan of a man with previous health problems in the chest.

Fig 24. Body scan of subject with overall network of red in body, indicating possible generalized nervous condition or circulatory problem or systemic infection.

Disclaimer: No Psychic Revelations or Imagery or attempts at revelations are intended in any way to be used by anyone for medical diagnosis and/or treatment. Only a medical professional is qualified to diagnose and/or treat medical conditions.

Images and Interpretations

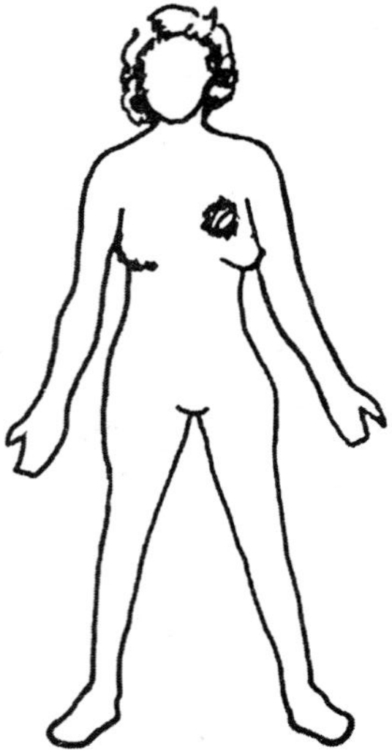

Fig 25. Body scan of woman with yellow mass, left breast, indicating chronic problem in left breast, but not life-threatening.

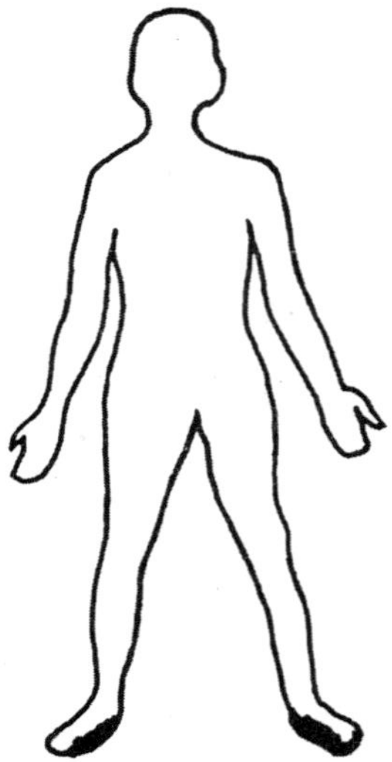

Fig 26. Health scan of man revealing redness on soles of feet—indicating current pain in the feet.

Disclaimer: Please see earlier page. All readings must be taken in context and are no substitution for Medical diagnosis and/or treatment.

Images and Interpretations

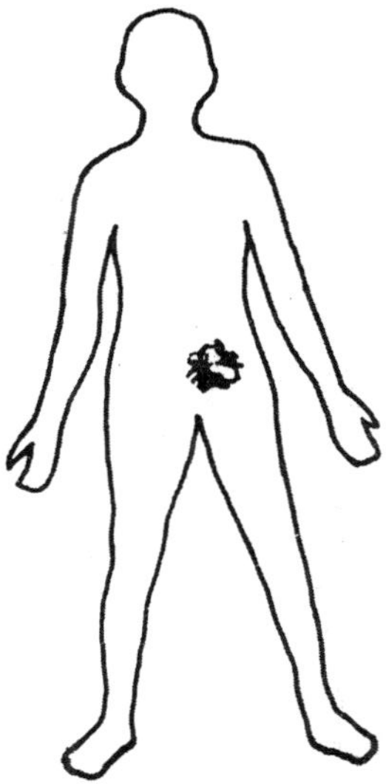

Fig 27. Body scan revealing red, indicating an active condition in abdominal area.

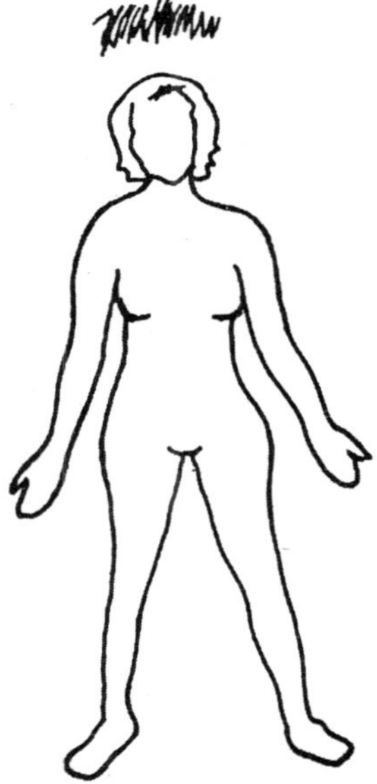

Fig 28. Body scan revealing area of redness at top of subject's head, indicating a possible recent head bump or injury or mental confusion.

Disclaimer: Please see earlier page.

Conclusion

In conclusion, we have seen that we can do psychic readings through the techniques described under "Mind Frames" and "Mental Posturing" via imagery similar to that depicted in examples from "Images and Interpretations". By so doing, we can read the lifeline past, present and future of a subject. We can give the subject information regarding health, finances, future relationships as well as present relationships, information regarding friends, relatives, business situations, etc. We can use this information in many ways for personal benefit, positive improvement and guidance.

We can, through positive imagery, seek desired goals in the future and can work to psychically insert these positive attainments on our lifeline.

In the final analysis, the ultimate goal for each of us is to be more informed, more positive, more successful in our relationships and our financial circumstances. Through the power of our psychic abilities, we can strive to make choices which are important for our happiness and success in all areas and for increased benefit and productivity to others and ourselves.

May these techniques and principles be utilized always for positive attainment and betterment.

BOOKS OF RELATED INTEREST FROM NAB

THE MAGICAL POWER OF PENDULUM: Focusing Your Energy for Self-Improvement & Psychic Development —*Richard Webster*

This book teaches you how to use a pendulum to help you make choices, locate lost objects, resolve health problems, communicate with spirits, explore past lives, identify self-imposed negativity, find a job, make decisions, set goals—and more. When you're ready for more advanced magic, in the twelfth chapter you will learn about Huna, the little-known methods practiced by the Hawaiian Kahunas to create magic and miracles.

ISBN: 978-81-7822-254-7

HEALTH FROM NATURE: The Ultimate Guide to Physical and Mental Well-being —*Tillman, Wolf, Hudson, Holden*

Health From Nature actually contains five different books which all have one thing in common: using nature for our physical and mental health. The book instructs the reader about the nature and use of vitamins, natural minerals, medicinal herbs, Bach flower remedies, and aromatherapy essential oils.

ISBN: 978-81-7822-246-2

THE ART OF GETTING WELL: A Five-Step Plan for Maximizing Health When You Have A Chronic Illness —*David Spero*

The Art of Getting Well is written to inspire and help people who are overcoming illness and want to improve their quality of life. Far more than just another list of recommended behaviors and attitudes, it explains how to change the very things in your life that contribute to illness and rob you of motivation in the face of chronic condition.

ISBN: 978-81-7822-288-2

AN ASTROLOGICAL GUIDE TO HEAL YOURSELF: Herbs, Health Foods and Your Zodiac—*Ada Muir*

Rediscover an ancient healing tradition and design your personal plan for health. *An Astrological Guide to Heal Yourself* unites two of the Earth's oldest traditions; herb lore and astrology in the modern incarnation. A simple and comprehensive guide to manage health at your own level. Learn ways to safeguard health by using natural products available through the bounty of nature. Blending herbs and astrology together, learn ways to prevent or even heal illnesses.

ISBN: 978-81-7822-230-1

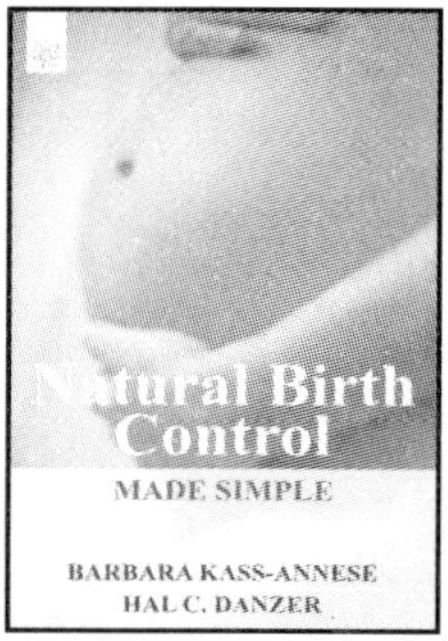

NATURAL BIRTH CONTROL: Made Simple

—*Barbara Kass-Annese, Hal C. Danzer*

Natural Birth Control Made Simple is an up-to-date guide to a system of choice in reproduction that has been around, in one form or the other, for thousands of years. It shows women how to recognize and chart their fertility signs, which indicate when they are infertile and can have sexual intercourse without conceiving or are most fertile and most likely to conceive.

ISBN: 978-81-7822-292-9

THE MAGICAL POWER OF HERBS: An Encyclopedia (Over 400 herbs described)

—*Scott Cunningham*

The Magical Power of Herbs contains the folklore and magical properties of over 400 herbs. Far from concentrating on esoteric, unobtainable plants, many of those mentioned within are old friends. The magical properties of onions, cashews, apples, rice, lettuce—as well as dill, basil, fennel, garlic, and parsley are described. Extensive tables, a cross-reference of folk names, glossary, and annotated bibliography make this a comprehensive and valuable guide to the practice of magical herbalism.

ISBN: 978-81-7822-277-6

INDIAN PHILOSOPHY A-Z —*Christopher Bartley*
This alphabetical handbook defines and explains key concepts in classical Indian philosophy, identifies controversial issues, describes major traditions of thought, and locates influential thinkers in their intellectual and religious contexts. They introduce the central concepts of the various branches of philosophy written by established philosophers, covering both traditional and contemporary terminology.

ISBN: 978-81-7822-313-1

BUDDHISM AND JUNGIAN PSYCHOLOGY:
—*J. Marvin Spiegelman, Mokusen Miyuki*
This book speaks about Jung's views on Tibetan Buddhism, India and Yoga, Chinese Taoism, Eastern meditation and Zen Buddhism, Western rationalism and Eastern Spirituality, how to integrate East and West. *Buddhism and Jungian Psychology* presents the findings, both personal and impersonal, of two Jungian analysts who have been propelled, by fate and psychic trajectory, to take up the encounter with the "other"

ISBN: 978-81-7822-115-1

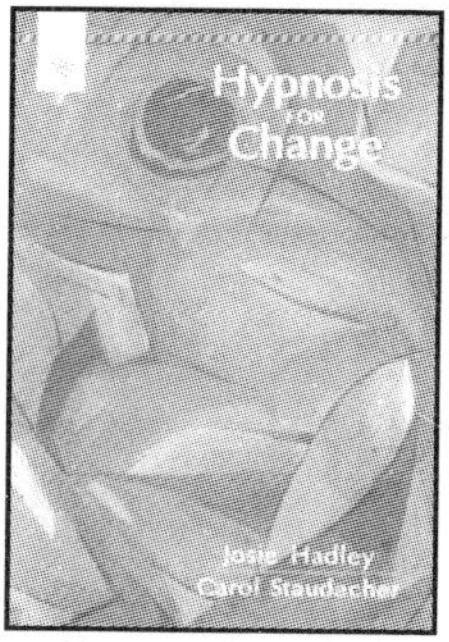

HYPNOSIS FOR CHANGE —*Josie Hadley, Carol Staudacher*
It gives an idea about the hypnosis and exploring all the facets examines the various aspects of hypnotic communication. It helps in overcoming the stress, anxiety and panic and treats specific phobias and improving your overall performance. The book discusses topics most relevant to people, identifying major problem pin points other trouble areas exacerbating that problem. It stresses that hypnosis can be amazingly effective and often is directly responsible for major changes in an individual's life pattern but it is not a guaranteed method of chasing away private demons.

ISBN: 978-81-7822-029-1

PSYCHIC POWERS: A Practical Guide—*Melita Denning, Osborne Phillips*

This practical guide offers complete step-by-step instructions on developing your innate psychic skills in divination, dowsing, clairvoyance, psychometry and spirit communication. This will enable you to positively change your life and the lives of those around you. It is a classic and comprehensive guide for awakening non-physical perception and make you utilise as yet untapped powers of mind.

ISBN: 978-81-7822-051-2

THE ART OF BLISSFUL LIVING —*B.B. Puri*

The *Art of Blissful Living* is the latest contribution by the author, Prof. (Dr.) B.B. Puri, after an overwhelming response to his earlier books. This book has made an excellent effort to establish the fact that Vedantic knowledge is based on fundamental principles in creating and maintaining a proper balance between body, mind, soul & environment with the help of Vastu Shastra, which is not merely an art but a definite science in itself. *The Art of Blissful Living* is based on the Spiritual Laws of Vedic Philosophy. By reading this book more and more people will benefit mentally, emotionally, physically and spiritually by adopting the Vedic Culture in line with the laws of Nature.

ISBN: 978-81-7822-307-0

THE INNER LIFE —*Charles W. Leadbeater*

The talks which comprise this book, *The Inner Life* were given to students of Leadbeater and Annie Besant, his close associate and fellow clairvoyant. Leadbeater assumed that his audience was thoroughly familiar with his enlarged world view. In this new edition it seems necessary to sketch out some of the main features of this view, to make the book more comprehensible.

ISBN: 978-81-7822-316-2